# THE EMANATED SCRIPTURE OF MANJUSHRI

## THE TSADRA FOUNDATION SERIES
### published by Snow Lion, an imprint of Shambhala Publications

Tsadra Foundation is a U.S.-based nonprofit organization that contributes to the ongoing development of wisdom and compassion in Western minds by advancing the combined study and practice of Tibetan Buddhism.

Taking its inspiration from the nineteenth-century nonsectarian Tibetan scholar and meditation master Jamgön Kongtrül Lodrö Tayé, Tsadra Foundation is named after his hermitage in eastern Tibet, Tsadra Rinchen Drak. The Foundation's various program areas reflect his values of excellence in both scholarship and contemplative practice, and the recognition of their mutual complementarity.

Tsadra Foundation envisions a flourishing community of Western contemplatives and scholar-practitioners who are fully trained in the traditions of Tibetan Buddhism. It is our conviction that, grounded in wisdom and compassion, these individuals will actively enrich the world through their openness and excellence.

This publication is a part of the Tsadra Foundation's Translation Program, which aims to make authentic and authoritative texts from the Tibetan traditions available in English. The Foundation is honored to present the work of its fellows and grantees, individuals of confirmed contemplative and intellectual integrity; however, their views do not necessarily reflect those of the Foundation.

Tsadra Foundation is delighted to collaborate with Shambhala Publications in making these important texts available in the English language.

# The Emanated Scripture of Manjushri

---

*Shabkar's Essential Meditation Instructions*

Shabkar Tsogdruk Rangdrol

TRANSLATED BY

*Sean Price*

FOREWORD BY THE

*Seventh Shechen Rabjam Rinpoche*

INTRODUCTION BY

*Matthieu Ricard*

SNOW LION
BOULDER
2018

Snow Lion
An imprint of Shambhala Publications, Inc.
4720 Walnut Street
Boulder, Colorado 80301
www.shambhala.com

9 8 7 6 5 4 3 2 1

First Edition
Printed in the United States of America

♾ This edition is printed on acid-free paper that meets the
American National Standards Institute z39.48 Standard.
♻ Shambhala makes every effort to print on recycled paper.
For more information please visit www.shambhala.com.

Snow Lion is distributed worldwide by Penguin Random House, Inc.,
and its subsidiaries.

LIBRARY OF CONGRESS CATALOGING-IN-PUBLICATION DATA

Names: Źabs-dkar Tshogs-drug-raṅ-grol, 1781–1851, author. | Price, Sean, 1968– translator.
Title: The emanated scripture of Manjushri: Shabkar's essential meditation instructions /
Shabkar Tsogdruk Rangdrol; translated by Sean Price.
Other titles: 'Jam dbyaṅs sprul pa'i glegs bam. English
Description: First edition. | Boulder: Snow Lion, 2018. | Series: The Tsadra Foundation series |
Includes bibliographical references and index.
Identifiers: LCCN 2018011718 | ISBN 9781559394611 (hardcover: alk. paper)
Subjects: LCSH: Spiritual life—Buddhism. | Buddhism—China—Tibet Autonomous Region—
Doctrines. | Mañjūśrī.
Classification: LCC BQ7805 .Z32513 2018 | DDC 294.3/444—dc23
LC record available at https://lccn.loc.gov/2018011718

For Ven. Konchog Tenzin

BUDDHA SHAKYAMUNI. PHOTOGRAPH COURTESY OF
VEN. MATTHIEU RICARD/SHECHEN ARCHIVE.

# CONTENTS

# FOREWORD

Shabkar Tsogdruk Rangdrol was the perfect example of a dedicated and accomplished practitioner who became an authentic master and vastly benefited beings. Born in the northeast region of Amdo, he attended teachers of all schools of Tibetan Buddhism and consequently spent years putting their teaching into practice; dwelling in hermitages, remote caves, and even on a distant island in the Blue Lake (Tso Ngönpo). He traveled far and wide throughout Tibet, meeting many of the great masters of his time, practicing in sacred places; he even made the daring pilgrimage through the Ravines of Tsari and traveled as far as Mount Kailash in western Tibet. He visited Nepal and gilded the pinnacle of the revered Jarung Khashor Stupa at Boudhanath, near Kathmandu. His teachings are known to be remarkably clear and profound. He would deliver them through spiritual songs, like the famous yogi Milarepa, or through his writings that fill fourteen volumes, which were published by Shechen Publications.

Like my grandfather and root master, Kyabje Dilgo Khyentse Rinpoche, Shabkar was an upholder of the nonsectarian approach (Rimé), which endeavors to ensure the preservation and transmission of the teachings of the various lineages of Tibetan Buddhism, also known as the Eight Chariots of Accomplishment.

I am therefore delighted that my dear friend Gelong Tenzin Jamchen (Sean Price) has brought to completion the translation of the *Emanated Scripture of Manjushri*, a text that explains the graded path of Buddhism through clear and inspiring pieces of advice—ready to be put in practice by anyone who aspires to enter the path of liberation.

May these teachings benefit countless beings and fulfill the compassionate aspirations of our spiritual masters.

The Seventh Shechen Rabjam Rinpoche, Gyurme Chökyi Sengye

# Introduction by Matthieu Ricard

When, in the early spring of 1814, Shabkar arrived at one of the most sacred mountains of Tibet, Mount Kailash, the "Silver Mountain," he had made up his mind—nothing else mattered but to engage in one-pointed spiritual practice. He wasted no time and within a few days, he collected some provisions and settled in a cave near the Cave of Miracles, where Milarepa had stayed seven centuries earlier. After singing some verses in praise of the holy mountain and of the great Lake Manasarovar, he sealed the entrance to his cave with mud and vowed to practice with complete dedication.

This cave lies a few minutes' walk slightly above and on the side of Milarepa's cave. To enter the cave, which is below the ground level, one has to descend a few steps. Since this cave is not as famous as Milarepa's dwelling (upon which a small temple has now been built), only a few pilgrims know about its location. Consequently, it has been left as it is, and it seems as if Shabkar had just left. The hearth where he used to boil his tea is still there, and an atmosphere of utter simplicity reigns in this secluded retreat place.

This cave is also located near the famous White Footprint, one of the four footprints said to have been left by Buddha Shakyamuni when he traveled miraculously to Mount Kailash. In fact, Tsogdruk Rangdrol ("Self-Liberation of the Six Senses," the name given to Shabkar by his root master Chogyal Ngakyi Wangpo, became known as "Shabkar," or "White Foot," in part because he spent many years near the Buddha's footprint, but also because wherever he would set his feet, the land would become "white with virtue," meaning that through his teachings, the minds of the people would be turned toward the Dharma.

While the great yogi was in strict retreat in this cave, not seeing or speaking to anyone, one of his heart-sons, Jimba Norbu, as well as quite a few other disciples, settled in the vicinity to practice near their beloved teacher. One day, through the curtain that was covering the small window made in the mud door sealing the entrance of the cave, Jimba Norbu fervently requested Shabkar to grant all of them some teaching.

The hermit asked himself, "Should I strive to reach perfection myself, or to help others?" With this question in mind, he prayed intensely to his masters and all the wisdom deities. One night soon thereafter, Simhamukha, The Wisdom Dakini with the Face of a Lion, appeared to him slightly before dawn and uttered a prophecy: "Indeed, it would be wonderful if through spending your whole life in practice you attained the body of rainbow light, but in doing so you'll be of little help to others in this lifetime. Now, is the time for you to bring many fortunate beings onto the path of liberation from samsara!"

Accordingly, Shabkar began to give teachings through the little window in the door of his cave, and continued to do so daily.

Later, after Shabkar had come out of retreat, hundreds of disciples— renunciates as well as faithful men and women—came from various places to hear his teachings, and for several years Shabkar turned the Wheel of the Dharma for their benefit.

At Mount Kailash, Shabkar wrote two of his major treatises, *The Emanated Scripture of the Kadampas*, which expounds the essence of the Buddha's teachings, as well as *The Emanated Scripture of Manjushri*. The latter, which has been translated in this volume thanks to the dedication and skills of Gelong Tenzin Jamchen (Sean Price), documents some of the requests made over time by various disciples and is written in the form of question and answer. Shabkar says in his autobiography that when he gave the reading transmission and some explanation of these two texts over several days, rainbows appeared in the sky, flower-shaped raindrops fell, and the atmosphere was filled with extraordinary fragrances. He felt "that the sky was filled with celestial beings who had come to attend the teachings."[1]

*The Emanated Scripture of Manjushri* is quite unique in Tibetan literature, not only because of its being written in the form of questions and answers, alternating verse and prose, but because it is a compendium of short teachings that presents a limpid, concise, and yet profound instruction on the entire graded path to enlightenment. It does so in a nonsectarian manner typical of Shabkar's approach. This graded path takes us first through a thorough presentation of the "mind training" (*Lojong*) teachings, based on Je Tsongkhapa's Great Graded Path (*Lam rim chen mo*), to pith instructions, essential teachings on the nature of mind according to the Mahamudra tradition of Milarepa, practical explanations on the songs of realization, or dohas, of Saraha, and culminates with the ultimate teachings of the Great Perfection, Dzogchen, the pinnacle of the Nine Vehicles.

Thus, in twenty-three pieces of advice, Shabkar elucidates the essentials of spiritual practice: the need to renounce the world, to rely on a spiritual master, and to unite meditation on emptiness with compassion. He explains how to meditate, how to apply in daily life the insights thus gained, and how to mingle one's mind with the guru's mind and liberate thoughts as they arise. Shabkar's style is crisp and effective, as if he had intended to define each step of the contemplative life in the briefest yet most complete and inspiring way for practitioners.

*The Emanated Scripture of Manjushri* opens with verses of praise to Lord Buddha, Padmasambhava, Atisha, and Tsongkhapa. Bringing together these four objects of devotion reflects Shabkar's whole life of practice.

Shabkar was born in 1781 among the Nyingmapa yogis of the Rekong (Reb gong) region in Amdo, the remote northeast province of Greater Tibet. At the age of fifteen, he recited Padmasambhava's mantra, "Om Vajra Guru Padma Siddhi Hung," one million times and had auspicious dreams, such as of flying through the air, seeing the sun and moon rising simultaneously, finding jewel-treasures, and so forth. "From then on," he wrote, "by the grace of Guru Rinpoche, I became filled with intense devotion to the guru, affection toward my Dharma friends, compassion for sentient beings, and pure perception toward the teachings. I had the good fortune to accomplish without obstacles whatever Dharma practice I undertook."[2]

He then met Jamyang Gyatso, a most respected Gelukpa master, whom he venerated greatly and of whom he later had visions and dreams. At the age of twenty, he received full monastic ordination and went into a prolonged meditation retreat, during which he let his hair grow long again, as was customary for retreatants. As a sign of having accomplished various yogic practices, he wore a white shawl rather than the traditional red shawl, although he continued to wear the patched lower robe characteristic of a fully ordained monk.

Shabkar then left his native land behind and traveled south of Rekong to an area called "Little Mongolia," a district in Amdo where a small Mongolian population had settled. Here he met his main teacher, the dharma king Ngakyi Wangpo, a learned and accomplished Mongolian king, said to be an incarnation of Marpa the Translator.

Having received complete instructions from his master, Shabkar practiced for many years in various hermitages and caves, including three years on the island of Tsonying, the "Heart of the Lake," in the Kokonor, the Blue Lake of Amdo. There, among other signs of accomplishment, he had a visionary encounter with Je Tsongkhapa.

Later, toward the end of his life, Shabkar had a vision of Padmasambhava. During the vision, Shabkar told Guru Padmasambhava that he had prayed to him throughout his life and had been blessed by visions of many other deities and spiritual masters. So why would Padmasambhava appear to him only now? Guru Padmasambhava replied, "Do you remember when, on the island of the Heart of the Lake, you had a vision of Tsongkhapa, who gave you the teaching on the Graded Path? That was I." In another of his writings, *The Emanated Scriptures of Orgyen*, Shabkar recounts this vision, and he expresses his faith in the inseparability of Guru Padmasambhava, Atisha, and Tsongkhapa.

While the core of Shabkar's practice was the Great Perfection, this practice was firmly grounded in the precepts of the Kadampa masters, which inspire practitioners to have few needs and desires; authentic feelings of renunciation, humility, and inner calm; loving-kindness; compassion; and, above all, the precious bodhichitta—the altruistic resolve to free all sentient beings from suffering and bring them to enlightenment.

Shabkar did not mince his words for practitioners who fool themselves by bypassing some steps of the path, out of childish impatience or arrogance:

> These days, some people say, "There is no need to expend great effort on the preliminary practices. What's the point of so much complication? It's enough just to practice Mahamudra, devoid of all elaboration." Don't listen to such nonsense. How can someone who hasn't even reached the shore talk about the sea?

In this spirit, *The Emanated Scripture of Manjushri* is a perfect companion for those who understand the need to progress step by step, rather than jumping all over the place at the risk of falling apart whenever confronted with outer, inner, and secret obstacles.

In thus uniting the teachings of the great Kadampa masters with those of the quintessential Nyingma tradition, Shabkar was a noble embodiment of the nonsectarian tradition that flourished in the nineteenth century, under the inspiration of other great luminaries such as Jamyang Khyentse Wangpo, Jamgon Kongtrul, Patrul Rinpoche, and Lama Mipham Gyatso.

Shabkar did not merely receive teachings from all the traditions of Tibetan Buddhism, he actively taught pure perception and open-mindedness. Moreover, he eloquently elucidated how all the many different Dharma teachings of the various *yanas* (vehicles) form one coherent whole. My root teacher,

Dilgo Khyentse Rinpoche, used to say that understanding the teachings of all Buddhist traditions to be noncontradictory is the sign of true knowledge.

The distinctive characteristics of Shabkar's works include directness, simplicity, profundity, and the power to encourage the reader to engage in spiritual practice. He does not write to flaunt his knowledge or to gain fame as a philosopher, but rather to turn readers' minds toward the Dharma, sustain their enthusiasm, and prevent them from becoming sidetracked or falling into the pitfalls that lie along the path to liberation.

After Mount Kailash, Shabkar went on pilgrimage to Nepal, where he gilded the pinnacle of the Jarung Khashor Stupa in Boudhanath and practiced in retreat in the secluded place of Lapchi, at the Nepal-Tibet border. Then he spent some time in Lhasa and Central Tibet, and, finally, in 1828, at the age of forty-seven, he returned to Amdo, where he tirelessly helped others through his extraordinary compassion. He spent the last twenty years of his life teaching disciples, promoting peace in the area, and practicing meditation in retreat at various sacred places, primarily at his hermitage in Tashikhyil.

The story of Shabkar's life as well as his teachings thus illustrates the complete path of Buddhist practice. He demonstrates the exemplary path of a perfect practitioner: having become disillusioned with worldly activities, he seeks a spiritual master, develops confidence in him, and follows his instructions. By practicing with complete dedication, in the end he himself becomes an enlightened master capable of contributing immensely to the welfare of other beings.

Shabkar left numerous writings, which I have humbly attempted to catalog, under the guidance of learned scholars.[3] In the present extent of our knowledge, no less than 180 compositions have been accounted for. As a result of the collaboration between the holders of Shabkar's lineage and our team at Shechen Monastery, almost all have been gathered. We found them chiefly in the valley of Rekong in Amdo as well as in various locations in Central Tibet and Nepal. A complete edition of Shabkar's collected writings was input at Shechen Monastery in Nepal and printed as a fourteen-volume set by Shechen Publications in India. A twelve-volume edition, prepared by Shabkar's fourth and present incarnation, Urgyen Jigme Tenpa'i Gyaltsen (born in 1980), was published in Qinghai.

Among his main writings, Shabkar composed three Dharma Discourses (*Chos bshad*) and three Excellent Discourses (*Legs bshad*), three Spiritual Instructions (*gDams nag gsum*), three Songs on the View (*lTa ba'i mgur*),[4] which include one of Shabkar's most renowned compositions, *The Flight of the Garuda* (*mKha' lding gshog rlabs*), composed on Tsonying Island when Shabkar was twenty years old, and nine Emanated Scriptures (*sPrul pa'i glegs bam*). The earliest of these is *The Emanated Scripture of Manjushri* ('*Jam dbyangs sprul pa'i glegs bam*), SH 55 in our catalog, composed around 1815, and the last one, composed around 1846, is also Shabkar's last major work, *The Emanated Scriptures of Compassion* (*sNying rje sprul pa'i glegs bam*), which opens with a beautiful hymn in praise of compassion, and continues with two sections in which Shabkar—a fervent defender of the "other" sentient beings, animals—condemns uncompromisingly the consumption of meat by Buddhist practitioners. To this, one should add a large autobiography, a shorter one that covers the last years of Shabkar's life (which mostly includes songs and teachings), and three large volumes of spiritual songs (*mGur 'bum*), as well as numerous miscellaneous writings.

As Shabkar reminds us in this volume, "If your practice of emptiness is devoid of compassion, you have not found the supreme path." The great yogi's life story as well as the teachings presented in *The Emanated Scripture of Manjushri* are constant reminders that what is not accomplished for the sake of others is not worth undertaking. All the while that we dedicate ourselves to free others from suffering and bring them to inner freedom, we should continually act within the understanding that, in the words of Shabkar, "Mind is the source or origin of all phenomena, both animate and inanimate, that are included within samsara and nirvana; failure to recognize this is called ignorance."

I am extremely grateful to Gelong Tenzin Jamchen (Sean Price) for kindly offering to the eyes and minds of countless readers and dharma practitioners this inspiring and accurate translation of these most precious teachings, a translation that was accomplished with great enthusiasm and consummate skills. May the merit of this commendable work be dedicated to the present and ultimate benefit all sentient beings without exception.

# TRANSLATOR'S INTRODUCTION

Shabkar Tsogdruk Rangdrol[1] (1781–1851) was born among the yogins of Rekong in Amdo. At a young age, he clearly demonstrated a strong tendency toward the spiritual life and sought out and received many Buddhist teachings. He developed a close relationship with his spiritual masters as he diligently put their instructions into practice,[2] driven as he was to live a truly spiritual life. Despite the repeated requests of his mother for him to live life as a married *ngakpa*, a lay tantric practitioner, which was common in Rekong, he declined, stating clearly that he wished to renounce the world and spend his life in a solitary spiritual pursuit. His mother eventually relented, and having received her blessing, Shabkar traveled to an isolated retreat site in Tashikhyil. There, at the advice and urging of his dharma friend Gyal Khenchen Rinpoche, he received full monastic ordination from Arik Geshe, Jampel Gelek Gyaltsen.[3]

It was during this time that Shabkar's life changed dramatically, for Gyal Khenchen Rinpoche suggested that he seek out the Nyingma master Chogyal Ngakyi Wangpo—a minor king in the Kokonor region. This suggestion awakened a latent tendency in Shabkar and upon hearing the name of his master to be, he longed to be in his presence. A short while later, Shabkar accompanied Gyal Khenchen Rinpoche, and they set out for Urgeh to meet the dharma king.

The meeting between Chogyal Ngakyi Wangpo and Shabkar proved to be auspicious, and the very next day the dharma king came into Shabkar's tent and began teaching him Tsongkhapa's *lam-rim* ("stages of the path") text *The Great Treatise on the Stages of the Path to Enlightenment*. The teaching and transmission, which given to Shabkar alone, took a month to complete. The reason for giving this particular teaching was made clear to him: the dharma king said, "I am glad that you have come here with the intention of practicing the Dharma. Having developed a bit of renunciation, one may turn to practice, but there is the danger that later the mind might change. So, to train your mind by studying and contemplating this text is very important." Shabkar then spent two months in the presence of his guru refining his understanding.[4] However, the real integration with the lam-rim took place after Shabkar left Little Mongolia and took up residence in Thayenchi, the Hermit's Meditation Cave, set within the pleasant solitude of Tseshung Grove.[5] Shabkar clearly states in his autobiography that while performing the preliminary practices and the famed accumulations there,[6] and for some time thereafter, his main practice was meditation upon *The Great Treatise on the Stages of the Path to Enlightenment*:

> For my main practice I trained with great perseverance in the whole of the *Graded Path of Enlightenment*. Thus I laid the foundation for an intense spirit of renunciation, of Bodhicitta, and a perfectly pure view.[7]

Shabkar's main practice was the Great Perfection, the pinnacle of Vajrayana Buddhism; however, his meditation was, as we have seen, firmly grounded in the Stages of the Path. He used these stages time and again to keep his own practice on the right track and, more important, for those of us who draw inspiration from him and his writings, he used them to guide his disciples—a guidance that we can connect with through his writings.

*The Emanated Scripture of Manjushri* is one such writing. We can contemplate the questions asked by his disciples in the light of our own attempts at Buddhist meditation, and it is as if Shabkar is replying to us directly—speaking to us across the centuries. His compassionate yet profound answers, given with great clarity and simplicity, guide us gently back to the path of genuine Buddhist practice. It is essentially a commentary on the Stages of the Path of Buddhist sutra and tantra—as such, it truly follows the entire path as per the intent of Atisha, one of the seminal figures in the lam-rim tradition.

Atisha was born in 982 CE to the royal household of Vikramanipura, Bengal. He was the second of three sons and named Candragarbha. By all accounts, he had a happy childhood—however, his life took a serious turn when at the age of eleven, on the eve of his wedding, he experienced a vision of the Buddha Tara, who advised him to flee the trappings of royal life. He did so and found himself practicing the teachings of Buddha in remote and lonely forests. He later received monastic ordination and was given the name Shri Dipamkarajnana, but he is renowned as Atisha. The king of Purang, Lha Lama Yeshe O, dismayed at the state of Buddhism in Tibet, invited him to the Land of Snows in the hopes of bringing about a sort of

Buddhist renaissance. Having received both the invitation and a prophecy from his yidam, the female Buddha Tara, to the effect that should he undertake the journey to the Land of Snows, he would never again return to the subcontinent and it would undoubtedly shorten his lifespan, but that, as far as benefiting the teaching of the Buddha was concerned, his sacrifice would be unparalleled, he decided to go.

Traveling through Nepal and into Tibet, Atisha taught the fundamentals of Buddhism and tried as best he could to correct the many misconceptions about the myriad styles of Buddhist practice that abounded in Tibet at the time. He spent several years teaching in the Tolung region. It was during this time that Atisha met the great translator Rinchen Sangpo. The famous account of their meeting mentions that at first Atisha was so impressed with Rinchen Sangpo's learning that he is said to have told Rinchen Sangpo that there was no need for him to come to Tibet. However, when Rinchen Sangpo proceeded to show Atisha the various seats he used for different Buddhist practices—clearly demonstrating that he didn't know how to integrate the different Buddhist practices into a single path—Atisha chastised him and called him a rotten translator!

These encounters, coupled with the request by Jangchub O, the nephew and successor of Lha Lama Yeshe O, prompted Atisha to compose a synthesis of his teaching, *A Lamp for the Path to Enlightenment*, written, as requested, in a style that Tibetans would find comprehensible and easy to put into practice. This short practice manual that lays out the stages of the path to enlightenment might have been what Tara was referring to in her prophecy when she affirmed that Atisha's travel to Tibet would be of immense value to Buddhism. Indeed, this little book has had a profound impact on the way Buddhism came to be practiced in the Himalayan traditions—an impact that is still felt throughout every Tibetan Buddhist tradition, each of which has produced numerous works of every genre on the subject, from poems to large instruction manuals. The Stages of the Path, a veritable step-by-step approach to Buddhist practice, remains Tibetan Buddhism's mainstay.

*A Lamp for the Path to Enlightenment* is an instruction manual belonging to the lam-rim or Graduated Stages of the Path genre. *Lam-rim* could just as easily be translated as "Stages of Realization." While having the connotation of a gradual experience, the term *lam* also refers to realization—that is, the stages of realization. The lam-rim is a contemplative's manual; it lays out a series of meditations that enhance and sustain Buddhist practice.

As Tsongkhapa wrote in *The Great Treatise on the Stages of the Path to*

*Enlightenment*, Atisha's *Lamp for the Path* is comprehensive and fundamental. Since it teaches by drawing together the key points of both the Sutra and Mantra vehicles, its subject matter is comprehensive; since it emphasizes the stages of disciplining the mind, it is easy to put into practice; and since it is adorned with the instructions of two masters (Atisha's teachers Serlingpa and Avadhutipa, followers of Asanga and Nagarjuna, respectively), it is superior to other systems.

*A Lamp for the Path to Enlightenment* begins by making clear the intentions or motivations of three types of individuals: persons of a lesser, middling, or greater capacity for spiritual practice.

Persons of lesser capacity are deemed to be those who have trust in the general or basic teachings of the Buddha: those dealing with past and future lives, the causal continuum of consciousness, the karmic law of cause and effect, and so forth. They act within an understanding of karma to generate positive potential, or merit, that will prove useful at a later date. In other words, there is no "renunciation" of samsara here. Persons of limited capacity are simply those who recognize cause and effect and do what they can to lessen the pain of contaminated existence.

Persons of middling capacity see through both the pleasure and pain of samsara and decide that no matter what the experience, it is ultimately of the nature of *dukka* ("suffering") and does not deliver any lasting satisfaction. Such persons reject outright the idea of samsara as holding any pleasures at all. They renounce or seek to emerge from that state of conditioned existence and achieve the state of liberation.

Persons of greater capacity are those who have engaged in the former two contemplations and found both to be flawed. The former leaves the contemplative in samsara, while the latter is limited—it does not result in the final awakening of buddhahood. The motivation of persons of greater capacity is to realize this potential and strive for it, inspired foremost by the thought of awakening not only themselves but rather all sentient beings.

This framework, characteristic of Atisha's *A Lamp for the Path to Enlightenment*, isn't found in every lam-rim. For example, the earlier lam-rim texts that Guru Rinpoche and Lady Tsogyal concealed in Tibet, in the eighth century, as texts to be revealed in the future (spiritual treasures or *terma*), texts such as *The Stages of the Secret Mantra Path*,[8] revealed by Nyang Ral Nima Oser[9] in the thirteenth century, or the more recent *Essence of Wisdom: Oral Instructions on the Stages of the Path*,[10] revealed by Chokgyur Lingpa and Jamyang Khyentse Wangpo[11] in the nineteenth century are clearly lam-rim texts—that is, guidance or instruction manuals that lead a practitioner in stages through the contemplative practices of Sutra and Mantra, but, generally speaking, they do not directly emphasize three distinct types of persons. Nor, for that matter, do the various manuals of the Stages of the Buddha's Teaching (*ten-rim*).

These Stages of the Buddha's Teaching texts are comprehensive manuals within which the Buddha's teaching of Sutra are presented in their entirety, but unlike Atisha's *Lamp for the Path*, the themes and practices of Tantra are barely hinted at. On the whole, the ten-rim manuals, found primarily in the Kadampa lineage of Atisha, follow the same patterns and themes. The most well known are those of Drolungpa[12] and Gampopa.[13]

It is interesting to note that the Kadampa masters used the two terms *lam-rim* and *ten-rim* for what is essentially the same thing: a compendium of the Buddha's teachings laid out in such a way as to make their understanding, contemplation, and meditation easily accessible. There is the suggestion that while the ten-rim lays out the way the teaching should be given, the lam-rim is slightly different in that, being a meditation manual, it changes the order of a few of the contemplations for ease of practice. Another difference is that while Atisha's *Lamp for the Path* covers the entire Buddhist path of Sutra and Tantra, ten-rim manuals deal exclusively with Sutra.

In any case, the two forms were amalgamated when, in the fourteenth century, Tsongkhapa composed *The Great Treatise on the Stages of the Path to Enlightenment*. As he wrote in the colophon:

> I have not cited anything from Atisha's *A Lamp for the Path to Enlightenment* aside from merely indicating the broad definitions of the three types of person. Instead I took as my basis the arrangement of the father and son—the great translator Ngok and Drolungpa.

*The Great Treatise on the Stages of the Path to Enlightenment* is a huge work of profound importance. It provides Buddhist practitioners with everything they need to build a secure and stable foundation upon which to start and sustain a solid practice of meditation and progress to awakening. As Tsongkhapa wrote in his dedication:

> May this treatise on the stages of the path to enlightenment, well founded on the wondrous deeds of the Buddhas and Bodhisat-

tvas, bring dignity to the minds of those who desire liberation, and serve to sustain the Buddha's activity.

The contemplations of the lam-rim are presented in a way that is meant to encourage, enhance, and sustain meditation practice. Indeed, the greatness of the lam-rim is indicated by four qualities it elicits in its practitioner:

1. Knowing that all of the Buddha's teachings are free of contradiction
2. Coming to understand that all of the scriptures are instructions for practice
3. The intent of the Buddha is easily found
4. The contemplative automatically refrains from the great wrongdoing of abandoning the teaching or instruction of the Buddha

These four qualities are of particular interest in the case of Shabkar. In a sense, it could be said that they defined his life: he received and practiced teachings from masters of all Tibet's Buddhist traditions; he spent his entire life in practice, focused upon the goal of awakening for the benefit of all; and he never rejected a single Dharma instruction. Throughout his autobiography, Shabkar tells us that he returned to the lam-rim time and time again. In his writings, we see how he took great care in the gradual training or gradual leading of his disciples. Indeed, the notes by his student Trulshik Orgyen Namgyal entitled *A Ladder for the Fortunate to Climb to Liberation* perfectly records the gradual style in which Shabkar taught; a style we find similarly recorded in *The Emanated Scripture of Manjushri*.[14]

Having grown increasingly weary of the world and, above all, with teaching—seeing it all as a pointless distraction—Shabkar decided to spend the rest of his life in solitary retreat. He decided to stay in an isolated spot and left for Mount Kailash. Once he had begun his retreat, many faithful men and women, monastic and lay alike, gathered in his vicinity; they too hoped to give their lives meaning by practicing the Buddha's teachings. Led by Shabkar's close disciple Jimba Norbu, they repeatedly asked Shabkar for teaching and instruction. Shabkar prayed to the deities of the Three Roots, "Should I leave my solitary retreat or lift the boundaries slightly and teach?" In reply, one night a little before dawn, Simhamukha, a wisdom dakini with the face of a lion, appeared before him surrounded by a large retinue of dakinis and urged him to teach. In accordance with this command, Shabkar began teaching through a small window in the door to his cave.

*The Emanated Scripture of Manjushri* is largely a record of these dialogues between Shabkar and his disciples. Traditionally, when, after much mutual checking and scrutiny of one another, a bond of trust is formed between a guru and disciple, it becomes the guru's task—their job if you like—to skillfully lead their disciples along the path to genuine spiritual accomplishment. This involves not just the giving of a teaching or instructions but also supervising the implementation of these instructions by the disciple. The process of integration, struggles with the practice, the transformation of one's mind through the practice, and so forth, are all then offered by the disciple to the guru. They will be discussed, and if the disciple has gone astray—fallen prey to misconceptions, erroneous understanding, self-deception, and so on—they will be skillfully guided back onto a genuine spiritual path. If progress is genuine, they will then be guided further. As you might imagine, this sort of relationship is extremely close and personal, but it is the only way that genuine progress along the entire spiritual path can be made.

In the twenty-two dialogues of *The Emanated Scripture of Manjushri*, Shabkar kindly affords us a glimpse into this kind of relationship. He shares the discussions he had with his disciples—the questions they had, troubles and difficulties they faced, and so forth. In answering their questions, it is as if Shabkar is speaking to us directly, helping us address the difficulties we ourselves experience in our own Buddhist practice. In all cases, it is with great compassion and consummate skill that he guides us back onto the path. We feel enriched and inspired.

The work concludes with Shabkar urging practitioners to avoid a sectarian or partisan bias—to embrace the Buddha's teaching as a whole and to refrain from the great wrongdoing of abandoning the teaching or instructions of the Buddha. Shabkar's advice is not about "becoming nonsectarian" but rather about looking beyond the packaging of the instructions and getting to the core—their practical application. To do this is to find inspiration in every aspect of the Buddha's teaching—to learn it, understand it, and above all to meditate upon it, which is another way of saying to practice and realize it for ourselves.

## ACKNOWLEDGMENTS

Initially, I must thank H. H. the Dalai Lama, who opened my eyes to the brilliance of the entire stages of the path over many years of both public and private teaching. Those instructions were subsequently refined into profound meditation instructions by Kyabje Denma Locho Rinpoche and Gen Namgyal Wongchen. These were later enhanced through the discourse, erudition, and instruction of Kyabje Trulshik Rinpoche, Shechen Rabjam Rinpoche, Benchen Tenga Rinpoche, and Sangye Nyempa Rinpoche.

Ven. Matthieu Ricard gave me a copy of *The Emanated Scripture of Manjushri* in the late 1990s, along with his encouragement to read the writings of Shabkar. He later inspired a sort of renaissance of interest in Shabkar by gathering and publishing Shabkar's collected writings in fourteen volumes.[15] Those of us who have benefited or been inspired by this great adept and his writings owe much gratitude to Matthieu. Indeed, it was Matthieu who first suggested that I translate the present volume. His dedication, devotion, and service to Shabkar, his writings, and lineage is quite extraordinary. I'd like to thank Matthieu for these, for the many other kindnesses he's shown me over the years, and for the inspiration he's given me as both a monastic and a disciple.

I must mention the kind assistance I've received from Yongzin Khen Rinpoche, Yeshe Gyaltsen and Thrangu Khenpo, Karma Gendun, both of whom gave much of their time for clarification, elucidation, and explanation of specific points in the text. I'd also like to thank Alak Zenkar, Khenpo Gyurme Tsultrim, and Lama Yonten Pasang for their help; Nick (of time) Schmidt for help with Sanskrit and other obscure language titles; Rafael Ortet for the beautiful art and so much more; Nikko Odiseos at Shambhala Publications; Michael Wakoff at Shambhala Publications for his editing and patience; and last, but by no means least, Eric Colombel, and everyone at Tsadra Foundation.

# The Emanated Scripture of Manjushri

GURU RINPOCHE. PHOTOGRAPH COURTESY OF
VEN. MATTHIEU RICARD/SHECHEN ARCHIVE.

# Opening Homage and Prologue

Homage to the Guru Manjughosha

Churned by Mount Meru, the maker of waves, the ocean of the two
  accumulations gave rise to the bright, stainless sun of the major and
  minor marks.
Youthful Siddhartha—victorious emanation kaya—
You rise like a sun for the glory of those to be tamed in this threefold
  world;
Your brilliance clears away the darkness of confusion and causes lotus
  buds of benefit and bliss to bloom.

The wish-fulfilling jewel of your teaching, mighty and majestic, is the
  source of all joy.
Thoroughly cleansed of all traces of ignorance, misunderstanding, and
  distortion—through explanation, debate and composition—it was
  mounted at the top of a victory banner.
When the offerings of hearing, thinking, and meditation are made,
  accomplishments, both common and extraordinary, will shower down.

Manjushri and Maitreya, heirs to the eradicator of spiritual poverty;
Nagarjuna, Asanga, and the rest—masters and adepts of India, you are all
  worthy of homage!
Like wish-granting gems, your amazing teachings have fully relieved the
  poverty of both samsara and nirvana.

Subsequently the dharma king, translators, and scholars endured many
  hardships to gather them here in the snowy land of Tibet.
Reflecting on their kindness, who could remain unmoved?

Padmasambhava, the great master who achieved the deathless vajra kaya;
Incomparable Atisha, keeper of the treasury of Buddha's teachings;

And, Omniscient Lobsang Drakpa, surely you are the second Buddha!
Each of you came and increased the teachings, source of benefit and bliss;
You also gave comfort and happiness to beings.
Reflecting on your kindness, who wouldn't wish to imitate you?

Having opened the jewel casket of instructions, you have been most
    generous with the contents.
Precious teachers, you have been kinder to me than the Buddha himself.
Allow me to offer you the accomplishment of my practice!

As the time of our demise is uncertain, I have accordingly prepared an
    opulent feast of the wondrous teachings I have received through the
    kindness of my Gurus.
Fortunate children of my heart, respectfully enjoy it!

These words praising the sublime gurus are offered as welcoming flowers.
To elucidate them a little:

    As the five degenerations raged, our sublime guide rose to the challenge.[1]
Donning the extraordinary armor of heartfelt resolve, he became known as
the incomparable Siddhartha. Among the buddhas of this fortunate age, he
is widely renowned as the White Lotus. His fame has reached the borders
of space itself and extended beyond the confines of existence. He turned the
profound and far-reaching dharma wheels innumerable times, filling the
world systems of the ten directions as if with light. His extraordinary teachings, likened to a wish-fulfilling gem, were received by his dharma heirs,
Maitreya and Manjushri, who in turn passed them on to their spiritual children, Asanga, Nagarjuna, and so forth—masters and adepts as innumerable
as stars in the sky at night! They, in turn, have continued to remove all traces
of ignorance, misunderstanding, and distortion by means of their explanations, debate, and compositions. Having presented the offerings of hearing,
thinking, and meditation to the pinnacle of the victory banner, they were
able to fulfill the wishes of future generations of disciples.

    The great dharma kings made it their life's work to invite numerous trans-
lators, scholars, abbots, and adepts to the snowy land of Tibet. These sublime
masters of the teachings have continually increased and spread happiness
and joy to all. Presenting the offerings of hearing, thinking, and meditation
to the pinnacle of the victory banner, they were able to halt the decline of
the Dharma.

Alas, that I haven't been able to act as they did! However, through the kindness of many qualified gurus, I do have a crown jewel to wear! In saying that, I am becoming old, and who knows for how long I'll be around? Consequently, I have decided to offer my fortunate disciples an opulent feast of the wondrous teachings that I have received from my masters.

ATISHA. PHOTOGRAPH COURTESY OF
VEN. MATTHIEU RICARD/SHECHEN ARCHIVE.

# I

# THE NECESSITY OF GIVING UP THE WORLD

During my sojourn at Mount Kailash, two of my fortunate disciples, the devoted, generous, and most intelligent dignitaries Lobsang Tsering and Wongpo, provided the necessities of life to both myself and the many retreatants there.

Subsequently, Lobsang Tsering renounced his life's concerns and came to join us. Offering me many provisions, he asked for instruction, "Lama Rinpoche, I am now old and close to death; please hold me in your compassion until I achieve enlightenment! In all my future lifetimes, may I never be separated from you, and may I continually come under your protection. Pray grant me instruction in the sublime dharma, with a special emphasis on retreat." He sang:

> Supreme lamp, clearing away the darkness of confusion,
> Supreme medicine, relieving the ills of the three poisons,
> Supreme jewel, fulfilling all wishes,
> Supreme gurus, so very kind—how wondrous you are!
>
> As Vajradhara, you abide in the nonmanifest realm,
> But to us ordinary folk, you appear as the lordly Tsogdruk Rangdrol.
> Precious guru, unceasingly kind,
> I submit infinite acts of homage at your lotus feet,
> Present you with countless offerings, confess all my downfalls,
> And rejoice in the actions of your body, speech, and mind.
> Pray turn the dharma wheel for us all!
> Continually remain among us and pass not into nirvana.
> To that end—to the longevity of the lama—I dedicate my merit—
> May it serve to increase your activities!

Glorious and precious guru, kindly pay me heed!
Throughout my entire life, I have consumed the poisonous waters of
    wrongdoing.
At the time of my passing, aside from the lower realms,
There will be nowhere else for me to go.

Now that my youth is already spent and death is upon me,
The fear of my demise urges me to practice the Dharma.

From now on, and in all future lives,
May I follow you, my protector, and never be parted from your side.
Pray grant me inspiring instruction for practice
And the strength to follow this through.

I replied, "If, from the very depths of your being, you wish to practice the
pure Dharma, you must practice in accordance with the example set by the
perfect Buddha and perpetuated by a stream of accomplished gurus, up to
and including your own root master. Initially, it is necessary to abandon the
concerns of this life. If these are not put aside, not only will it be difficult for
you to practice perfectly, you will also fall prey to negative actions, suffering,
and reproach. *The Collected Sayings of Potawa* say:

> The sign of not practicing the Dharma is not having renounced
> this life.

Shawopa remarked:

> When the concerns of this life are many, we may feel ill at ease,
> wander around, and the three—negative action, suffering, and
> reproach—strike simultaneously.[1]

Geshe Tonpa once asked Atisha, 'Please explain the results of action
motivated by thoughts of this life's happiness, personal gain, and renown?'
The elder replied, 'Just that.' 'What, then,' he continued, 'will occur in the
future?' 'The realms of hell, of hungry spirits, and of animals,' came the reply.
    "Abandoning the concerns of this life, all the happiness, well-being, and
renown of the dharma, samsara, and nirvana will simultaneously occur. *The
Collected Sayings of Potawa* mentions:

In learning harmonics, initially the sound 'ei' is a difficult note to master but with perseverance it becomes easier. Similarly, when beginning to practice the Dharma, the initial abandonment of the concerns of this life is hard. However, once this is done and with continual practice, it becomes easier.

The Buddha said:

> If you desire every bliss,
> Thoroughly abandon all your desires.
> By giving up desire,
> Supreme bliss is won!

Togden Samten Pel remarked:

> To desire the happiness of this life brings suffering.
> Cast your desire to the wind!
> For then permanent happiness will be won.

Kyechok stated:

> From the moment you desire nothing,
> Your renown will pervade the earth.
> From the moment you devote your life to the Dharma,
> The cool breeze of your renown will stir.

Moreover, in the sutras, it is stated:

> The exhaustion of desire is the actual state of a noble one—
> To weaken desire is to abide in their lineage.

And *The Initial Mind Training Instructions* says:

> It is preferable to have abandoned desire than to possess the renown of Buddha.

Moreover, at the time of his passing, the peerless Atisha was asked by the yogi Chakpa Trichok, 'After you have passed, should I devote myself to meditation?' Atisha replied, 'If it is a negative action, give it up!' The yogi continued, 'Well then, should I just teach?' Again, the same answer was given. Again he asked, 'Should I divide my time between meditation and teaching?' Once again, Atisha gave him the same answer. Finally, the yogi asked, 'What should I do?' 'Give up the concerns of this life,' Atisha replied.

"Giving up the concerns of this life is the entrance to the Dharma. Rigpa'i Wongchuk said:

> Unless you pursue the practice of Dharma single-pointedly,
> To simply assume you are a practitioner is foolish indeed; how sad!
> The first practice is to abandon the concerns of this life,
> Check thoroughly to see if you have done so.

The Dharma is not only important at the start; it is critical at the beginning, the middle, and at the end of your practice. Please keep this in your heart! Yangonpo said:

> I held the abandonment of the concerns of this life to be the core of my accomplishment.

All the great ones have spoken thus.

Should you wonder, 'Has my practice of Dharma been genuine or not? Will it become genuine Dharma or not?' you need to investigate whether or not you have given up your obsession with the comforts of life, such as your homeland, friends, relatives, your food, wealth, and so forth. If you have not done this, you are not truly practicing the Dharma and, as such, you will not gain any genuine experience. If, on the other hand, you have relinquished your obsession, your practice is genuine and will prosper in the future.

"When taking his leave, Milarepa received the following advice from Marpa: 'Child, if you neglect to abandon worldly concerns but rather mix them with the sublime dharma, that will be the end of your practice.' *The Collected Sayings of Potawa* states:

> Just as you cannot make both clothes and a water carrier from just one animal skin, it is impossible to work for both this and your future lives. Just as you must choose to make either clothes or a water carrier, similarly, you must choose to work for the prosperity of this life or for the dharma of your future lives.

The Precious and Great Pandita of Sakya said:

> Unless the pride of obtaining the comforts of life is relinquished any
> hope of attaining the everlasting happiness of liberation is a fool's
> wish, a mere pretense.
> Therefore make an effort to abandon the concerns of this life and
> accomplish enlightenment.

And from the Dharma Lord, Gyalse:

> No one can accomplish both the concerns of this life and the
> sublime Dharma;
> Those desirous of realization should have no doubt as to which path
> is misleading.

"If you are wondering just what needs to be given up in abandoning the
concerns of life: you need to let go of your obsession with your homeland,
friends, relatives, fellow countrymen, household, food, wealth, possessions,
and body. The way to abandon them is just as the masters of the past have
taught: with the four aims, the three vajras, as well as these three: the casting
out, the pursuit, and the achievement. I shall explain these as follows. The
four aims are as follows:

> Aim your heart toward practicing the Dharma.
> After this, aim to practice as a beggar.
> As a beggar, aim to practice until you die,
> And until that time, aim to frequent lonely ravines.

The three vajras are as follows:

> Place the unwavering vajra before you.
> Leave the vajra of contemptibility behind,
> And carry the wisdom vajra with you.

And the three, the casting out, pursuit, and achievement are as follows:

> To be cast out from human society;
> To pursue the company of dogs;
> And, to achieve the status of the divine.

These are called 'the ten innermost jewels.' Merely bringing them to mind causes the collapse of the fortress of destructive emotions. It causes the destruction of the ship of negative actions, allowing you to reach the blissful shore of the antidote. Once you possess these ten innermost jewels, there is no doubt that you will swiftly and effortlessly achieve every comfort, in both this and in all your future lives. I sang:

I supplicate the Buddha, the kind gurus, the direct and lineage masters!
Please bless me to act as the past masters have done, and to abandon
    the concerns of this life!

Previously the peerlessly fine son of Shuddhodana witnessed illness,
    aging, and death and was deeply moved.
Renouncing his princely status, he wandered to the banks of the
    Neranjana.
There he engaged in austerities and six years later awakened and
    became Buddha.

Similarly, all sublime masters of the past contemplated
    impermanence and their own demise.
Becoming forlorn, they abandoned the concerns of their lives, left
    to practice in lonely places, and became enlightened in a single
    lifetime.
Similarly, by reflecting on the uncertainty of death,
Why shouldn't I abandon the concerns of this life?
Concern for my homeland, home, fields and friends, relatives,
    possessions, food and wealth; all these are ill-suited toward a pure
    practice of the dharma.

Aside from the necessities of life,
Three robes, a begging bowl, and such like,
I shall not keep anything more—no gold or jewels—
Nothing for my own welfare shall I possess.

My death is certain, and at that time wealth, friends, and so forth, are
    of no help.
What's more, if they are with me, the suffering of separation will
    arise—
Thinking thus, I shall abandon my obsession with this life.

I'll aim my heart toward practicing the Dharma,
I'll aim to practice as a beggar,
As a beggar, I'll aim to practice until I die,
And, until that time I'll aim to frequent lonely ravines.

I'll place the unwavering vajra before me, and, leaving the vajra of
    contemptibility behind, I'll carry the wisdom vajra along with me.

Becoming an outcast from human society,
I'll take lowly positions and dress in rags.
Pursuing gladly the company of dogs,
I'll achieve the ranks of all the gods.

In essence then, everything is impermanent and death will swiftly
    come.
The time to abandon the desires of this life has come!

Through the blessing of the gurus and the force of my own virtue,
May I be able to relinquish the concerns of this life!

If this is recited and its meaning contemplated, you will quickly be able to
renounce the concerns of this life."

# 2

# How to Rely upon a Spiritual Teacher
## *A Ninefold Perception*

---

My fortunate disciples Sonam Topchen and Ngawong Chodrup, both of whom are inclined toward the Dharma, asked me, "Precious master, everlasting refuge, the sutras, tantras, and pith instructions all speak of the importance of perfect reliance upon a fully qualified spiritual friend as the source of all spiritual qualities. However, due to our confusion, we tend to miss the point! Pray tell us the correct way of reliance." They sang:

> Supremely wondrous and precious master,
> Emanated yogi, how amazing you are!
>
> Kind mother, you care for the wretched.
> Providing father, you instantly fulfill our wishes.
> Supreme guide, you reveal the path to liberation.
> Great eye, which teaches what to take up and abandon;
> Master, who liberates from the fears of the lower realms;
> Supreme healer, revealing the pain of the disturbing emotions;
> Supreme sun, benefiting all;
> Wish-fulfilling jewel, bestowing all that is asked for;
> Divine drum, beating the rhythm of the Dharma;
> Excellent vase, fulfilling all desires;
> Udambara flower, so hard to find;
> Buddha in person, so meaningful to behold;
>
> Perfect and precious master,
> Renowned as the lordly Tsogdruk Rangdrol;
>
> I understand how all the sutras, tantras, and pith instructions insist
>     that the basis of all qualities is perfect reliance on a kind teacher,
>     but I am unable to practice it.

Therefore with my palms folded in homage,
I request that you to grant me an instruction, both pithy and complete,
That clearly teaches the way to rely properly upon a spiritual friend.

From now on and in all future lives,
May I rely upon you, my spiritual friend.
Never tiring of drinking the elixir of your instructions,
May I come under your ripening and liberating refuge.

I realize that even if I were to search for hundreds of aeons in myriad
 fields, both pure and impure, it would be difficult to find a teacher
 such as you.

As such, I dedicate my merit that I might follow you,
And, until enlightenment, may I never be parted from you.

I replied, "*The Flower Ornament Sutra* mentions how you should serve
and respect your teacher with nine perceptions, and how all instructions for
relying upon spiritual teachers are included in these.

1. To have the perception of yourself as being like an obedient son:
   An obedient son doesn't play around doing whatever he likes but
   rather shows respect for his father and does what he is told. Similarly, give up your own agenda and continually give yourself over
   to the instructions of your teacher.
2. To have the perception of yourself as being like a vajra: The seven
   extraordinary features of a vajra are as follows: invulnerability,
   indestructibility, truth, solidity, stability, being unobstructed, and
   immutability. Similarly, when devils, negative friends and so on,
   try to come between you and your teacher by spreading lies and
   deceit, remain undivided like a vajra.
3. To have the perception of yourself as being like the earth: The
   earth is able to bear the burden of whatever is placed upon it. Similarly, you should accept and bear the burden of whatever your
   teacher gives you and exert yourself at it without tiring.
4. To have the perception of yourself as being like a mountain: A
   great mountain cannot be moved. Similarly, when receiving
   instructions from your teacher, you should be immutable, endur-

ing whatever unwanted difficulties, such as hunger and thirst, come your way.

5. To have the perception of yourself as being like a servant: When a king commands his servants to do something, they act. Similarly, when entrusted with your teacher's instructions, you must act on them and put them into practice without the slightest misgiving.

6. To have the perception of yourself as being like a sweeper: A lowly sweeper doesn't have any pride in his position. Similarly, you should hold yourself as being lower than your teacher, abandoning any ideas of being superior to him.

7. To have the perception of yourself as being like a rope: A rope can hold whatever it ties up. Similarly, you should joyfully adhere to your teacher's instructions no matter how difficult they may be.

8. To have the perception of yourself as being like a dog: A guard dog never gets upset with its master no matter how he is treated. Similarly, if your teacher belittles you, ignores you, scorns you, shouts at you, publicly exposes your hidden faults, and so forth, you must not get upset.

9. To have the perception of yourself as being like a boat: A boat never tires no matter how many hundreds or thousands of times it is taken out on the water. Similarly, no matter how much fetching and carrying your teacher asks you to do, you must remain without ever tiring of it.

"If you are able to respect and serve your teachers with these nine perceptions, even if you do not practice, qualities will naturally and spontaneously arise in you and you will complete a vast collection of merit, speeding you on to the perfection of buddhahood. I sang:

> Lordly masters, kinder than even the buddhas,
> Root gurus, I supplicate you!
> Pray bless me that in this and all future lives I shall be able to
>     respectfully rely on qualified teachers!

> Relying on a spiritual master is the root of all benefit and bliss,
> As well as being the basis of all good qualities;
> As such, even at the cost of my life, may I never abandon him,
> But rather rely upon him with the greatest of respect.

Respectfully entrusting myself to a qualified guru,
May I act like an obedient child, listening to and acting upon his
    instructions.

When demons, bad friends, and the like try to tear me away,
May I remain inseparable, steadfast, like a vajra.

When given the burden of the lama's work,
May I be like the earth, the bearer of all.

While relying on the lama, whatever difficulty occurs,
May I remain resolute, steadfast like a mountain.

While engaged in the most menial of tasks,
May I be undisturbed, like a servant deferring to royal patronage.

Having given up on pride and holding the guru as supreme,
May I act like a humble sweeper.

If the tasks given by the lama prove taxing,
May I be like a rope, joyfully holding them all.

If the lama belittles, ignores, or chastises me,
May I remain without anger, like a dog.

When the lamas send me on errands,
May I be like a boat, joyfully carrying them out.

Precious and glorious root guru, pray bless me to practice
    accordingly, and in this and all future lives, may I act with such
    devotion toward such gurus.

If you recite these verses aloud, while thinking over their meaning, you'll
have the fortune to perfectly devote yourself to spiritual friends in this and
all future lives."

# 3

# IDENTIFYING A PRECIOUS HUMAN BIRTH

*The Eight Freedoms and Ten Endowments*

My student Lobsang Tsultrim had given up the affairs of his life and was now focusing exclusively on his future lives. He asked me for a concise summary of the eight freedoms and ten endowments that comprise the valuable and precious human birth, by means of cause, examples, and numerical comparison, as found in Jamgon Lama Tsongkhapa's *The Great Treatise on the Stages of the Path to Enlightenment*, the great lamp of the teachings that dispels the darkness of confusion in the minds of all throughout the three worlds. He sang:

> Your explanation, debate, and composition all arise without
>     obstruction:
> Your explanations benefit your disciples,
> Your debates overcome your opponents, and your compositions
>     illuminate the teachings!

> Supreme among the learned of this decadent age,
> Field of merit for beings' homage and offering,
> You are a spiritual friend to all—
> Yogi, to merely behold someone like you is a cause of great wonder!

> Pray listen to me with loving concern:
> In my youth, I was preoccupied with meaningless activity,
> And wasted this precious life of leisure and freedom.

> With a sense of remorse, I pondered, and decided to make use of this
>     life and practice the dharma's essence;
> This led me to you—precious master—who unerringly teaches the
>     path to liberation.

Precious Guru, in accordance with *The Great Treatise on the Stages of the Path to Enlightenment,*
Kindly grant me a clear and concise explanation of the eight freedoms and ten endowments that comprise a precious human life—
Which is of great value and so very hard to acquire—
And, having considered them, of the need to extract its essence.

Foremost captain, pray navigate your passenger—my wretched mind—smoothly across samsara's deep and poisonous waters in the ship of a precious human life.

To safely dock at the city of permanent bliss, where the unpleasantness of birth, aging, sickness, and death don't exist; not even in name!

I replied, "The 'eight freedoms' are freedom from birth as a hell-being, a hungry ghost, an animal, a long-lived god, a person harboring wrong views, a savage living in the border regions, and a person with impaired senses or an imbecile, and freedom from birth at a time when a buddha hasn't appeared and taught. These are known as the eight states that lack freedom, for if you find yourself born in any of them, you won't have the freedom to cultivate virtue. We have found ourselves to be free from such experiences, as such, we have the freedom to engage in virtuous actions; we have the 'eight freedoms.'

"The five features conducive to practice are to be born human; in a central land that has the fourfold assembly;[1] with all your senses, such as your eyes and ears, intact; not having committed, or caused others to engage in, the extremely negative actions of immediate fruition and thereby not having an incompatible lifestyle;[2] and with faith in the sublime Dharma—the collections of ethical discipline and so on,[3] as the source of all benefit and joy. These pertain to you; as such they are known as the 'five individual endowments.'

"And there are five more: Buddha has appeared; taught the excellent Dharma; those teachings remain; have many followers; and there are those who genuinely care for practitioners, benefactors who provide food and clothing. These pertain to others; as such they are known as the 'five circumstantial endowments.'

TSONGKHAPA. PHOTOGRAPH COURTESY OF
VEN. MATTHIEU RICARD/SHECHEN ARCHIVE.

"These freedoms and endowments are of tremendous benefit. For example, a wish-fulfilling jewel can provide you with anything ordinary you might wish for, such as food, clothing, and so on, but it can't grant you the extraordinary accomplishment of buddhahood. However, if you utilize this precious human birth and practice the dharma, you can attain both the common and extraordinary accomplishments. The opportunity afforded through the possession of these freedoms and endowments far exceeds even the wish-fulfilling jewel.

"Just this once you have managed to obtain a life of freedom and endowment; even if you were to search among the myriad states of bondage for eighty thousand kalpas, to find its like again would prove most difficult, as indicated by the following:

1. Cause: The rarity of the coming together of an ethical lifestyle—which serves as foundation—supported by the engagement in charity and the other perfect actions and pure aspirations.
2. Analogy: The Buddha said it is more difficult to obtain a human life than for a turtle surfacing from a vast ocean's depths to put its head clean through the hole of a wooden yoke adrift on its surface. Moreover, if you were to throw dried beans at a smooth wall, very few would stick to it and most would fall to the ground. This is analogous to birth in the eight states lacking freedom, whereas the few that stick represent a human life of freedom and endowment.
3. Numerical comparison: It is said that there are as many beings in hell as there are particles of dust comprising the earth, as many hungry ghosts as there are grains of sand, as many animals as there are barley dregs in a brewer's barrel, as many gods and demigods as there are snowflakes in a blizzard, but that human lives with freedom and endowment are as few as the dust particles you can pile onto a fingernail.

"As you can see, a human life of freedom and endowment is rare indeed; if you happen across one, you must endeavor to make full use of it. Therefore think, 'I'm going to make the best possible use of this life of freedom and endowment!'" I summarized:

I supplicate my kind guru; pray bless me to be mindful of the
    difficulty of finding freedom and endowment.

To have the eight freedoms is to be free of eight restricting states:
Birth in hell, as a hungry ghost, an animal, or a long-lived god,
As one with wrong views, a savage dwelling in border regions,
With senses impaired or a fool,
Or at a time when a buddha has neither appeared nor taught.
To be born as a human; in a central land that has monks and
    others who make up the fourfold assembly; with complete
    senses—fivefold;
Faith in the Dharma, the Vinaya, and so forth, for the source of all
    benefit and joy;
And neither engaging in nor encouraging extreme negative action.
These make up the five individual endowments.

The Buddha, having both appeared and taught,
His teachings remaining and being practiced by those patrons who
    lovingly grant support—
Five aspects complete, make up five circumstantial endowments.

If, with this gem, a human life of leisure and endowment, I practice
    the sublime dharma,
Every accomplishment, both ordinary and sublime, can be mine—
Its greatness exceeds even that of a wish-fulfilling jewel.

I have it this once, and to gain another at some future time would
    prove most difficult,
Requiring the gathering of ethics, as foundation, charity and so forth
    as support,
As well as pure aspirations; causes, so rare!

As the Awakened One has taught us, to obtain a human life is about
    as likely as a blind turtle surfacing from the depths and putting its
    head cleanly through the hole in a drifting yoke.
By analogy, we can come to know its rarity.

And lastly to compare humans and others by numerical comparison:
Of the dust particles on a fingernail, so few, against those comprising
    the whole world, so many.
Through the comparing of numbers, we can understand how rare it is.

At this juncture, having obtained a human life so rare and of such
   great value,
I must strive to extract the essence of the sublime Dharma.

In brief, having won freedom and endowment—so rare and of such
   use—the time is now upon me to practice the Dharma.

Glorious and most precious root guru, pray bless me to seize this
   opportunity!

If you recite these verses clearly and dwell upon their meaning, a natural
wish to make use of your life and to really extract the essence of the Dharma
will arise from deep within.

# 4

# DEATH AND IMPERMANENCE

*Three Roots, Nine Reasons, and Three Conclusions*

---

I was asked by my fortunate disciple Jimba Norbu, one who cherishes the precious higher training in ethical conduct—the basis of all qualities—for a summary of the three causes, nine reasons, and three conclusions that comprise the chapter on death and impermanence from the unequaled entrance way for those striving for liberation *The Great Treatise on the Stages of the Path to Enlightenment*. He sang:

> Lama, I offer homage to your body, speech, and mind!
> Your body, composite of the buddhas of the three times,
> Your speech, which roars with the sound of all dharmas,
> And your mind of love and wisdom—so very hard to fathom.

> To consider one's mortality and impermanence,
> To give up the thoughts of this life,
> And to practice the sublime dharma are three practices to take up, so
>     they say.

> However, I grasp at permanence in such a way that when death
>     descends I won't be able to let go.
> In these and other ways I find myself preoccupied with the ways of
>     the world.

> I continually see others die,
> And, always hear you say "Nothing lasts!"
> But still, bad child such as I am,
> I hanker after the permanent!

> Yet, the youthful Manjushri in the guise of a human—
> The Dharma lord of the three worlds—

Composed an unparalleled book,
An incomparable and most excellent entrance way for those striving
    for liberation:
*The Great Treatise on the Stages of the Path to Enlightenment.*

Pray grant me a clear and concise summary of the methods with
    which to contemplate death and impermanence based upon the
    three causes, nine reasons, and three conclusions.

Precious and most qualified master,
Please bless me to be mindful of my mortality,
And ever mindful of death;
May I become free from the demon of grasping after permanence!

From now until attaining enlightenment, may I never be apart from
    you, my protector;
Tasting the nectar of your speech,
May I quickly attain omniscience.

I replied, "The first causal instruction for meditating upon death and
impermanence is to consider how death is certain. There are three reasons
to contemplate:

1. The lord of death is certain to come for you and nothing can turn
   him away. This holds true for all beings, regardless of their status and no matter how proficient they may be in ritual ceremo-
   nies, casting of spells, or dispensing of medicine. Whatever your
   strengths or means, you can do absolutely nothing to avoid death.
   Contemplate this until the utter conviction of your own mortality
   dawns.
2. Your life span cannot be extended; it just keeps on diminishing.
   Your food and wealth may increase and decrease, but not your lifetime. It is continually decreasing, and even the slightest extension
   is out of the question. Contemplate this until the absolute certainty of your own death dawns.
3. Convinced of your own mortality, even in the time you have left
   you still give little over to practice. Half of your life is spent in
   sleep. As a child, you didn't know how or forgot to practice, and
   when you are old even though you may remember to practice, you'll

be unable to. During your youth, you are continually distracted: making friends and fighting enemies, in business deals and other money-making ventures,[1] worrying over food and drink, given over to idle chatter, so much so, that even in light of the certainty of your own demise, your life is still wasted.

"These will lead to the first of the three certainties: death, the enemy of life cannot be stopped, and your meeting with him is inevitable. This will cause you to become disillusioned with the ways of the world and think only of practice. You'll become certain of the need to practice the dharma and will continually promise yourself to do so.

"The second causal instruction is to contemplate how the time of death is uncertain. Again, there are three reasons to contemplate:

1. The duration of any life span in our world isn't certain. Beings in other world systems have a fixed life span, however, beings of our southern continent of Jambudvipa do not.[2] Contemplate how the length of your own life is uncertain.
2. The causes of death are many while those that sustain life are few. Consider the uncertainty of your own life; it's like a candle flame in a storm. Amid manifold causes of death such as the 430 types of illnesses, the eighty thousand malevolent spirits, elementals, and so on, consider also how the causes that sustain life are very few indeed.
3. This illusory body of ours is extremely fragile, like a water bubble; meeting with the tiniest condition, possibly something you wouldn't even consider to be destructive, like a thorn prick, can easily serve as the circumstance of your demise. Thereby contemplate life's uncertainty owing to the fragility of your body.

"These contemplations will take you to the second certainty: since there is no certainty as to when the lord of death will destroy your body and life, examine what is really important and quickly make the decision that, besides dharma practice, nothing else is worthwhile; take a pledge to practice and recite it to yourself over and over again.

"The third causal instruction is to contemplate how, at the time of death, nothing besides your Dharma practice is of any value. Once again there are three reasons to contemplate:

1. When death comes to you, no matter how many loving and concerned friends and relatives are by your side, you cannot take even one of them along with you. As such, contemplate that at the time of your death your friends cannot help you.
2. At death, your possessions cannot help you. Imagine that you own heaps and heaps of jewels; when death comes for you, you won't be able to take the tiniest of gemstones with you.
3. Contemplate how you'll have to leave your own flesh and bones behind on your deathbed; at the time of your passing even your cherished body is of no use to you.

"And through their contemplation, you'll arrive at the third certainty: at the time of death the only protector, refuge, and guardian is your Dharma practice. All the enjoyments of the world will leave you behind and similarly you will leave them. As the time for your parting from the world isn't fixed, there's every chance it could happen this very night! With conviction, give up all your worldly activities and concentrate solely on practice. Certain of your commitment to practice, make a pledge to do so and repeat it to yourself time and time again." I sang:

> I supplicate at the feet of my kind root guru,
> Pray bless me to be mindful of impermanence and death!
>
> As there isn't a single person who has avoided death,
> An impermanent person such as I will surely die.
> For this very reason, Yama will defiantly come by;
> This visit cannot be avoided and will surely come to pass.
>
> There is nothing new to be added to my life span, which just keeps
>     on diminishing to my certain demise.
> Continually distracted with slumber, merrymaking, and more,[3]
> There's no time to practice divine Dharma, yet still I have to die.
>
> Having cast aside the meaningless activities of this life,
> Resolve to practice the sublime Dharma.
>
> Many die while young.
> Similarly, I too could suddenly die; nothing is certain!

If the life spans of this world aren't definite,
Then surely mine isn't fixed.
With manifold harm from illness, spirits, and enemies,
And so few things to help uphold and sustain life,
I'll definitely pass on!

This illusory body of mine is so very fragile,
The slightest thing can easily destroy it, and, at some unknown time,
    this will too come to pass.

Casting aside the meaningless activities of this life,
Surely the time to practice the sublime Dharma is right now!

When you are face to face with Yama, the terrifying lord of death,
Nothing besides the sublime Dharma is of any use.

No loving or concerned friends can accompany you—they are of no
    help!
That delightful money you've worked so hard for has to be left
    behind—it is worthless!
Even the very flesh and bones you were born with have to be left
    behind when, from your deathbed, you go on alone—
It's all useless!

Casting aside the meaningless activities of this life, surely it's time to
    practice the sublime and meaningful Dharma!

In essence, impermanence will swiftly usher in our demise,
And so the time to practice the divine Dharma is now upon us.
Precious and most glorious root guru,
Pray bless me with the capacity to practice the sublime Dharma!

If you sing these verses, while contemplating their meaning, you'll notice
your concerns with the world will diminish and your interest in the sublime
Dharma, the method for all future happiness, will naturally increase.

# 5

## BASIC ETHICS

*The Ten Virtuous Actions and Their Counterparts,*

*the Ten Negative Actions*

---

My disciple Khetsun Donden—one who is diligent in the threefold practice of study, contemplation, and meditation—requested a brief instruction: to recognize and abandon the causes for bad migration, the ten nonvirtuous actions, and the methods for achieving a fine rebirth replete with the eight characteristics of full maturation in the higher realms, the ten virtuous actions. He said my explanation should be given in accordance with the miraculous book *The Great Treatise on the Stages of the Path to Enlightenment*, a veritable composite of the eighty-four thousand dharmas in their entirety. He sang:

> You are honorable, untainted by impurities and defects,
> Skilled in the methods of subduing those to be tamed,
> And made ever excellent by your love, compassion, and bodhichitta.
> To meet a spiritual friend such as you—the very embodiment of skill,
> honor and excellence—is rare indeed!

> I pay homage and supplicate at your lotus feet, my protector.
> Kindly grant me, a man overpowered by delusion and karma,
> your attention:

> In my youth, I didn't even think of the Dharma,
> As I got older, I marveled at the monastery's wealth.
> Ever foolish, I obsessed over its increase and brought my monastic
> duties down to the level of worldly commerce.

> Ever blundering and foolish in so many ways—
> As the master Shantideva said:[1]

Not only have I avoided virtue,
I have amassed negative actions.
Surely for countless aeons to come,
I shall not even hear the words "higher rebirth."

Understanding this, I urged myself to cast negative action aside—
For, it's said, unless a fine birth,
Comprising all the characteristics necessary to actualize the supreme
    path, is won, progress will be slow.

Just so, the wish to practice the instructions of the victor Lobsang
    Drakpa was born in me.

Protector, pray give me a brief teaching—
One that clearly indicates the good actions to be taken up and the
    bad ones to be avoided—as indicated in *The Great Treatise on the
    Stages of the Path to Enlightenment*.

Instruct me how to thoroughly abandon the causes of bad rebirth,
    the ten negative actions,
And take up the causes that result in a birth possessed of the eight
    fruitions;
In your great kindness, please listen to my request!

Spiritual friend who teaches what to take up and what to avoid,
May I never be apart from you.
Practicing your instructions, abandoning negative actions,
And taking up virtue, may I win enlightenment!

I replied, "The causes of the lower realms, the ten negative actions, are as
follows. There are three physical negative actions:

1. To kill is to take the life of another sentient being, such as a human,
   a horse, a dog, a goat, a sheep and so on.
2. Stealing is to take another's possessions when they aren't freely given,
   be they gold, silver, jewelry, clothing, food, drink, and so forth.
3. Sexual misconduct is, for a layperson, to leave your partner and
   have sexual relations with another's and, for a monastic, to have
   any kind of sexual relationship.

"There are four verbal negative actions:

4. Lying is, for example, to say you have seen something that you haven't.
5. Divisive speech is to cause a rift between friends or associates.
6. To speak harshly means to verbally abuse others.
7. To gossip is to idly chatter and prattle on about nothing in particular.

"And there are three negative, mental actions:

8. Covetousness is a wish to possess another's possessions.
9. Harboring ill will is to desire to inflict harm on your enemies, and also to rejoice in another's endeavors to harm them.
10. Wrong view is a disbelief in action—cause and effect—the three jewels, and so on.

"If you engage in these actions on a vast scale, the result is birth in hell, a middling engagement results in birth as a hungry ghost, and a mild engagement results in birth as an animal. In each case, you'll have to endure unbearable sufferings.

"Just as you would stop eating certain foods once you have realized that they are harmful to you, know these ten negative actions to be the cause of rebirth in the three lower realms; it's essential to give them up.

"The methods of achieving a fine rebirth replete with the eight characteristics of full maturation are as follows:

1. The causes of a long life span are to avoid harming other living beings, to adopt a nonviolent attitude, to ransom the lives of animals about to be killed, and to nurse and provide medicines for the sick and needy.
2. The causes of clear complexion are to offer lights, such as butter lamps, as well as new clothing and beautiful jewelry.
3. The causes of a consummate lineage are to conquer pride, to offer homage to your gurus, and to treat others with the highest respect—as if you were their servant.
4. The causes of great influence are to be extremely charitable, giving your wealth and possessions to everyone—regardless of their financial position.

5. The causes of trustworthy speech are to avoid the four verbal negative actions.

6. The causes of renown as a great power are to make prayers to achieve various good qualities in the future, to make offerings to the three jewels, as well as to your parents, hearers, solitary realizers, abbots, masters, and gurus.

7. The causes for birth in a favorable situation[2] to practice the dharma are to delight in the merit of those who have such a circumstance, to shun and discourage actions that would lead to less favorable circumstances, and to rescue beings from castration.

8. The causes of strength are to do that which no one else has been able to, to assist on projects that require your help, and to give food and drink.

"To achieve a fine life of freedom and endowment, adorned with these eight characteristics of full maturation, will enable you to make extraordinary progress on the spiritual path. To this end, you must now exert yourself." I sang:

I supplicate at the feet of my kind masters;
Pray bless me to abandon wrongdoing and take up virtue!

Killing, stealing, and sexual misconduct;
Lying, divisive speech, harsh speech, and gossip;
Covetousness, ill will, and wrong view
Make up the ten nonvirtuous actions.
To engage in them is to cause bad rebirth, so abandon them!

For longevity, save and ransom life;
For a fine physique, offer lights and be patient;
To be born of a good family, be respectful to all;
For influence, be charitable to the destitute;
For your speech to be worthy of trust, abandon negative words;
To possess renown as a great power, make offerings and prayers;
For future birth in a favorable situation, prevent castration;
And for great power, offer others your assistance.

Acting like this, I'll come to achieve a fine life,
Adorned with these eight characteristics of full maturation,

And further spiritual progress can be made;
Just so, I'll apply myself right now!

In essence, by thoroughly abandoning the ten nonvirtues,
I'll have embraced virtue—
Glorious and most precious root guru,
Pray bless me with the capacity to give up sin and practice virtue!

If you recite these verses while thinking about their meaning, you'll naturally begin to give up negative action and take up virtue.

# 6

# THE DISSATISFACTORY NATURE OF SAMSARA

A disciple, Sonam Nyendrak, who, in his youth had given himself over to the world and now, in the latter part of his life, had achieved a sense of renunciation and an urge to practice the sublime Dharma, asked me for a general summary of the eightfold, sixfold, and threefold ways of contemplating the ultimately dissatisfying nature of samsara. In addition, he requested a specific reflection on the sixfold suffering experienced within the six realms of existence. He asked that the teaching be given in accordance with *The Great Treatise on the Stages of the Path to Enlightenment*—a veritable window into the entire teachings of the Buddha. He sang:

> Respectful homage to you, O master—
> You who lead beings from the lower realms,
> To the state of humans, and then on to the higher status of
>     buddhahood.
>
> I present you with all of these offerings amassed here,
> Admit my failings,
> Rejoice in virtue, request you to turn the Dharma wheel,
> Pass not into nirvana, but remain indefinitely!
> I dedicate all merit to the increase of your enlightened activity.
>
> Refuge in this and future lives, as well and that in-between—
> Root master, kindly pay me heed!
>
> The masters of the past have told us to become disenchanted with
>     the oceanic sufferings of samsara.
> However, I have been overpowered by confusion and emotion and
>     rather than become weary I have become rather addicted to it and
>     now view pain as pleasure.

Having now given rise to a sense of renunciation,
I request you, precious guru, in your great kindness,
Pray grant me a concise contemplative method upon which I might
　　strive for liberation.

Based upon Jamgon Lobsang Drakpa's *The Great Treatise on the
　　Stages of the Path to Enlightenment*—
That window into the entire teaching of Buddha—
Kindly elucidate the general eightfold, sixfold, and threefold
　　sufferings of samsara,
As well as the specific sixfold sufferings of the six types of being.

Having grown weary with samsara,
May I give up the affairs of this life and strive solely for liberation—
Pray bless me to succeed!

Until that state is won, please hold me close and sustain me with
　　your loving- kindness;
Through your compassion, O protector,
May I be liberated and achieve supreme bliss!

I replied, "To list samsara's eightfold suffering: the suffering of birth, aging, sickness, death, encountering that which is unpleasant—such as enemies— separation from that which is pleasant—like friends—unfulfilled desires, and lastly the sufferings of the contaminated aggregates, which serve as the basis for all former experiences of suffering and lead to future ones.

"The sixfold suffering is as follows: uncertainty—such as when friends become enemies and vice versa; insatiability—being unable to turn off your addiction to the pleasure of indulgence and the boredom of misery; repeatedly changing bodies—no matter what kind of form you have, be it superior, inferior, or somewhere in-between, it won't last and will eventually have to be cast away; of repeated rebirth—continually having to be born from a mother's womb; repeatedly changing your status—from king to beggar, and so on; and finally the suffering of being without the support of good friends/ companions and having to go on to your next life alone.

"The threefold suffering is as follows: the suffering of change—all plea- surable experiences within samsara are contaminated and sooner or later will turn into suffering; the suffering of continual suffering—the unbear- able physical and mental suffering, arising, for example, from aging, leading to illness and ultimately death; former suffering giving rise to future suffering, which in turn gives rise to yet more suffering; and the suffering of conditionality—whatever you can remember, or remember having done, or are planning to do, while you are under the influence of karma and the destructive emotions will be of the nature of suffering.

"As for the specific sixfold sufferings of samsara: essentially, beings in hell suffer from heat and cold; hungry spirits suffer from hunger and thirst; animals suffer from exploitation; humans suffer from birth, aging, sickness, and death; demigods suffer from quarrels; and gods suffer from death and transmigration.

"In essence, through the force of karma and destructive emotions, wherever you find yourself born within samsara, be it of high or low status, you'll find it to be a place of suffering. Whatever you enjoy will not provide you with any lasting satisfaction, and whatever you do will only fuel future suffering. This is why samsara is likened to a pit of fire, an island of cannibals, or a nest of vipers. Think of its pleasures as being like food laced with poison, a honey-coated razor, or the jewel on a poisonous snake's head—the merest touch of which will kill you—and you'll come to see how samsaric enjoyment is like being shown delicious food when you have a stomach upset. You will thoroughly give up your addiction to samsara and become like a prisoner freed from jail.

"Thus you'll directly realize the need to exert yourself in the practice of the sublime Dharma, the only way to free yourself from the great ocean of samsara, which is violently whipped up by waves of karma and destructive emotion and filled with terrifying crocodiles and other sea monsters—the three sufferings." I sang:

> I supplicate my kind guru; pray bless me to be mindful of samsara's
> suffering!
>
> All beings suffer from birth, aging, sickness, and death,
> Meeting with the unpleasant—enemies,
> Separation from the pleasant—loved ones,
> Not finding that which they desire,
> And the suffering of the five appropriated aggregates,
>
> The suffering of uncertainty between friend and enemy,
> A lack of satisfaction, repeatedly casting off of bodies,
> Being reborn over and over again from a mother's womb,

And the continual ascent and inevitable fall,

The suffering of being without companionship,
The sufferings of change, the sufferings of suffering itself,
And the suffering of conditionality—many sufferings indeed!

In particular: beings in hell suffer from heat and cold,
Hungry spirits suffer from hunger and thirst,
Animals suffer from exploitation,
Humans suffer from birth, aging, sickness, and death,
Demigods suffer from quarrels,
And gods suffer from death and transmigration.

Samsara is as a fiery pit, an isle of cannibals, or a snake pit.
Its delights are like food laced with poison,
A razor blade coated in honey,
Or like the jewel upon the dark head of a poisonous snake—one
    touch and you are finished—it seems needless to say!

In essence there is no lasting satisfaction within samsara,
And so the time to part company is upon me.

Precious and most glorious root guru,
Pray bless me to be free of my addiction to samsara!

Recite well these words clearly and contemplate their meaning. Before too
long, you'll come to find your obsession with the delights of samsara diminishing and being replaced with a natural, uncontrived wish to practice the
Dharma—the means to achieve the stable bliss of liberation.

# 7

# THE IMPORTANCE OF ETHICS

My disciples the fortunate Gendun Thosam and Samdrup Senge asked me for a brief instruction to help them keep pure morality and to elucidate the benefits of an ethical lifestyle. They sang:

> Previously, the son of Shuddhodana
> Took timely ordination and became the supreme monastic.
> Unshakable monk, you are not clothed in the stains of downfall,
> May I come to follow in your footsteps.
>
> Spiritual friend of us monastics,
> You have told us how the basis of all qualities is the precious higher
>     training in ethics,
> And, after having taken it up, of the need to prevent its decline.
> Time and again you have emphasized this, yet still we don't
>     understand.
>
> Therefore, precious master,
> Please grant us a concise teaching on the means and benefits of
>     keeping the vows that we've taken.
> And bless us, we pray, to guard the vows that we have taken as we
>     would our eyes.
>
> In all our lifetimes, may we never be apart from you, O protector,
> And may the higher training in ethics not decline,
> But continue to prosper!

I replied, "By reflecting on the sufferings of samsara such as birth and death, you'll come to view all of existence to be like a blazing forest fire. This will lead you to seek liberation—the taking up and adherence to the precepts of individual liberation, which is of great importance. *The Nirvana Sutra* says:

> Ethical discipline is the staircase for all virtue.
> Just as trees and the like are rooted in the earth, it's like a root.
> Just as the head merchant goes before all the other traders, ethics
>     goes before all the other virtues.
> Just as Indra hoists his banner in victory,
> Ethics is the victory banner of all dharmas.
> It severs the paths leading to the lower realms and all negative action.
> It is the medicinal herb that heals negativities' ills,
> The provisions for the long and terrifying path of life,
> The weapon that slays the enemy of delusion,
> The spell that cures the snake of the destructive emotions' poison,
> And a bridge across poisonous water.

*The King of Concentration Sutra* says:

> To consciously make offerings of food, drink, incense, banners,
> lamps, and flower garlands to myriad buddhas for as many aeons
> as you can find sand grains in the Ganges River—virtue indeed;
> however at the time of the destruction of the Dharma, when the
> Sugata's teaching is in decline, to keep a single precept for an
> entire day would be greater still.

*The Tantra Requested by Subahu* says:

> Just as every harvest grows without fault in dependence on the earth,
> So too do the highest virtues depend on ethics and grow by being
>     moistened with the water of compassion.

The protector Nagarjuna has said:

> Just as the earth is the basis for everything, be it static or in motion;
> Ethics, it's said, is the foundation of all qualities.[1]

"Protect your ethics as you would your very eyes. A lack of understanding is a gateway through which violations can occur, so study and learn your precepts well. Another is disrespect, so learn respect for the teacher, his advice, and those friends who observe pure morality. Yet another is carelessness, so become conscientious: give rise to mindfulness, self-respect, and modesty. Finally, entertaining too many disturbing emotions is a gateway through which violations may occur. In reliance upon their respective antidotes, crush them as soon as they arise. In essence, to live in pure morality means to strip off the clothing of wrongdoing." I sang:

> I supplicate at the feet of my kind masters,
> Pray bless me to guard ethics as I would my eyes!

> Ethics are like steps leading to liberation,
> Like the earth, they are the foundation for all qualities,
> Like a head merchant, they lead all other Dharma practices,
> Ethics are the very victory banner of the sublime Dharma.

> Ethics sever the pathways of negative action and those leading to
>     lower realms.
> Like a medicinal herb, they heal negativities' ills.
> Ethics are like provisions for life's terrifying journey,
> Or a weapon, with which to slay the enemy of delusion.

> Therefore, I shall protect, as I would my eyes, the precious higher
>     training in ethics!

> Unknowing is a gateway through which violations can occur,
> It can be avoided by knowing the precepts.
> Disrespect is another; respect for the precepts is the cure.
> Yet another is carelessness; this can be remedied with mindfulness.
> And finally, to be possessed of too much destructive emotion is a
>     gateway through which violations can occur.
> These can be done away with by the swift application of their
>     respective antidotes.

> In essence, to be naked and free of the garments of impropriety is to
>     live in pure morality.
> Precious and most glorious root guru,
> Pray bless me to guard the higher training in ethics!

Any merit ensuing over the three times I dedicate to the perfection
of ethics.
In this and all future lives, may I never be apart from the higher
training in ethics!

If you recite this and contemplate its meaning well, you'll come to have the
highest respect for ethical conduct.

# 8

# HOW TO ESTABLISH GENUINE COMPASSION

My disciple, the hermit Lobsang Tsultrim, asked me for a piece of profound advice—one he could practice continually. He sang:

Embodiment of all the victors' knowledge, love, and activity,
Who showers accomplishments, both common and supreme,
    in their entirety,
Root guru, Vajradhara, Tsogdruk Rangdrol, I offer homage at
    your feet.

I offer everything, actually arranged here and visualized,
Confess all my failings and rejoice in virtue.
I request you to remain for hundreds of aeons,
And continually turn the Dharma wheel,
And finally I dedicate all virtue, as exemplified hereby,
    to enlightenment.

The majesty of your body adorned with the major and minor signs,
The roar of your speech as it proclaims the eighty-four thousand
    bundles of teaching,
And your unobstructed mind of love and wisdom that knows all.
Thus I praise the master's body, speech, and mind!

Having achieved your own perfection, you effortlessly strive for the
    welfare of others,
Through the four means of gathering disciples.
Wish-fulfilling jewel who eliminates the poverty of this decadent
    age; homage to you—wish-granting master!

From now until I'm enlightened,
Whatever the situation, be it happy or sad, good or bad,

I have no hope other than you;
Pray accept me as your disciple, and keep me at your side.

Through reasoning, I have come to understand the teaching of Buddha,
And from my heart I have taken refuge in the three jewels.
With perfect adherence to what should be done and what not,
Pray bless me to practice as you have, O guru!

Pray teach me an instruction the simple hearing of which causes the
    Mahayana lineage to awaken,
Whose contemplation enables one to be counted among the
    bodhisattvas,
And through meditation thereupon one eases into buddhahood
    without the slightest interruption.

I shall not mix the supreme ambrosia of the guru's instructions with
    the poisonous waters of the eight worldly dharmas—both black
    and white[1]—
But aspire to practice them in solitude.
Pray bless me to accomplish this wish!

I replied:

You show equal and continuous love to the person massaging your
    right arm with fragrant sandalwood oils and to the one hacking
    away at your left with an axe.
O buddhas of the ten directions, I place the crown of my head at
    your feet.

With a compassion that doesn't tire,
You would, for the benefit of others, willingly remain in the fires of
    the incessant hells for an ocean of aeons.
O bodhisattvas, I respectfully offer homage to you

Seeing the misery of beings caused you to shed tears and gave rise to
    a great compassion such that you'd gladly sacrifice yourself to save
    them.
O lamas, most gracious and kind, to you I respectfully bow.

"The supreme and most extraordinary feature of Mahayana Buddhism is its root, precious compassion—a veritable wish-fulfilling jewel, source of the most marvelous qualities. I shall now explain the methods of its meditation, listen respectfully.

"Other spiritual traditions place less emphasis on great compassion, but it is, however, the unique feature of Mahayana Buddhism. It is the source of the extraordinary qualities of buddhas and bodhisattvas, the root of both the causal vehicle of the perfections and the resultant vehicle of secret mantra, the Vajrayana. For yogins of the Mahayana, great compassion is crucial at all times—in the beginning, middle, and at the end of practice.

"As the second Buddha, Tsongkhapa, wrote in his eloquent and unparalleled composition *The Great Treatise on the Stages of the Path to Enlightenment*, a lamp for all beings in the three realms:"

## THE IMPORTANCE OF COMPASSION IN THE BEGINNING

"Once your mind is moved by great compassion, you will definitely make the commitment to free all beings from cyclic existence. If your compassion is weak you will not. Therefore, compassion is important in the beginning because feeling responsible to free all beings requires great compassion and because if you do not take on this responsibility, you will not be ranked as a Mahayanist. As the *Teachings of the Aksayamati Sutra* read:

> Venerable Shariputra, should you wonder why the great compassion of the bodhisattvas is inexhaustible? It is because it is the prerequisite. Just as the movement of the breath is the prerequisite for the life of a human being, the great compassion of the bodhisattvas is the prerequisite for correctly reaching the Mahayana.

And from the *Foremost of Gaya Sutra*:

> "Manjushri, what is it that motivates the bodhisattva deeds? What is its object?" To which Manjushri replied, "Devaputra, great compassion motivates the bodhisattva deeds; its object is living beings."

"Thus compassion is the basis of engaging in the deeds because when you see that you will not live up to your commitment without training in the two vast collections, you will set about the difficult work of amassing these vast collections."

## THE IMPORTANCE OF COMPASSION IN THE MIDDLE

"You may develop the spirit of enlightenment at one time and then engage in the bodhisattva deeds. But when you see that living beings are innumerable and act improperly, that the training is very difficult and without limit, and that you need an immeasurable length of time, you may lose heart and fall into the attitude of the Hinayana. However, by accustoming yourself to increasingly greater compassion that is not just a one-time development, you become less concerned with your own happiness or suffering and are not discouraged at providing others' welfare. Therefore you easily accomplish all the collections.

Kamalashila's *First and Larger Stages of Meditation* reads:

> Because bodhisattvas are moved by great compassion, they diligently strive to be very helpful to others without considering themselves. Consequently, they engage in accumulating the two collections, which is very difficult, tiring, and requires a long period of time.

As the *Seal of Engaging in Developing the Power of Faith Sutra* reads:

> One who has great compassion will always take on a life of suffering and will always give up a happy life in order to help all living beings to mature.

"If bodhisattvas engage like this in something that is extremely difficult to do, they will fully and quickly complete the collections. They will definitely attain the high status of omniscience. Therefore the sole root of a buddha's qualities is compassion."

## THE IMPORTANCE OF COMPASSION AT THE END

"Based on the power of great compassion, buddhas, even when they reach their goal, do not abide in peace like Hinayana practitioners but continue to work for the welfare of beings as long as space remains. For without compassion, buddhas would be like shravakas. Kamalashila's *Middle-Length Stages of Meditation* says:

> Since the bhagavan buddhas are imbued with great compassion, they remain until the end of the realm in which beings dwell, even though they have attained the complete perfection of their own aims.

He also wrote:

> The sole cause of the nonabiding nirvana of the bhagavans is great compassion.

"The glorious Chandrakirti taught that just as seeds, water, and ripening are important in the beginning, middle, and end of a harvest, similarly compassion is important in the beginning, middle, and end of the harvest of buddhahood. His *Introduction to the Middle Way* reads:

> Compassion alone is regarded as the seed of a buddha's excellent harvest, as water is for its development, and the maturation is a state of long enjoyment. Therefore, at the beginning, I praise great compassion.

With this powerful idea in mind, the *Compendium of the Teachings Sutra* reads:

> Bhagavan, bodhisattvas should not learn many teachings. Bhagavan, if bodhisattvas grasp and know one teaching, they will have all the Buddha's teachings in the palm of their hand. What is this one teaching? It is great compassion.
> Bhagavan, with great compassion, all the Buddha's teachings are in the bodhisattva's palm. For example, Bhagavan, wherever the precious wheel of a universal sovereign is, there also is the assembly of his battalions. Likewise, Bhagavan, wherever the bodhisattva's great compassion is, there are all the Buddha's teachings. For example, Bhagavan, once there is a life force, all the other sensory factors will exist. Bhagavan, similarly, once

great compassion exists, all the other bodhisattva's qualities will appear.

Moreover the *Tantra of Vairochana's Enlightenment* reads:

Lord of Secrets, the Buddha's omniscient wisdom arises from the root of great compassion.

*The Bodhisattva Basket Sutra* reads:

Great compassion is that which goes before a bodhisattva's enlightenment.

*The Condensed Perfection of Wisdom Sutra* says:

Bodhisattvas naturally enter into an altruism that doesn't distinguish between beings—this is the teaching of great compassion, the spiritual vehicle of the victorious buddhas.

*The Array of Flowers Sutra* says:

While in the spring-like beauty of youth, the divine Norzangma said her compassion was as inexhaustible as an ocean, it removed the misery of all beings, and would ultimately result in her awakening—as it has done for all buddhas.

From the *Ornament*:

Initially the root and finally the supreme fruit; such is the development of the wish-fulfilling tree of compassion. If the root of compassion is missing, it will be difficult to endure the task.

And also:

Great compassion is the root of all qualities. Such compassion is focused on all sentient beings without exception; reacting to their misery with love transforms all into an immeasurable joy.

*The Question of Lodro Gyatso Sutra* reads:

> To awaken to buddhahood one needs but a single dharma: a compassion that isn't concerned with one's own comfort, a great compassion.

And to quote the oral tradition of mind training:

> As for the highest of offerings, there are three: bodhichitta, to hold the Dharma, and meditation upon compassion.

*The Sutra That Discriminates between the Paths of Virtue and Sin* says:

> Longevity comes from compassion.

*The Teaching of the Buddha's Sneeze* says:

> Compassion is the supreme offering; come to possess it!

"Geshe Tonpa (Dromtonpa) once inquired of a young monk as to where Khampa Lungpa (Drolungpa Lodro Jungne) was residing and what he was doing.[2] The little monk replied that he stayed in a small hermitage, his head covered, and was forever crying. Dromtonpa removed his hat and, placing his palms together at his heart, he wept. He said, 'That is truly amazing. He is a true practitioner. I could explain his many qualities to you, but he wouldn't like it!'

"As you can see, the principal practice of the followers of Atisha is great compassion. *The Book of Kadam* reads:

> Drom asked, "Precious Elder, many are greatly afflicted by disturbing emotions, pray grant an instruction to remedy this."
>
> Atisha replied, "Drom, altruism and compassion are the most important."
>
> "Precious Elder, altruism and compassion are important in all Dharma practices, aren't they?"
>
> The elder replied, "Drom, it is for that reason that I mentioned them. If altruism and compassion are missing, rampant concepts and thoughts cannot be tamed."

Drom then asked, "Precious Elder, you have extolled the great benefits of altruism and compassion; tell me, would a person with these qualities ever be affected by a contagious disease or a plague?"

Atisha said, "Drom, an individual, completely devoid of self-interest and infused with altruism would not be affected. Nor would he be affected by spells, black magic, evil mantras, the disdain of the *mamos*,[3] warfare, and so on."

"What is the cause of such a great altruism?"

"A fierce and extraordinary compassion."

Drom went on, "How does one begin to practice the four immeasurable attitudes in this tradition?"

Atisha replied, "Drom, when a compassion that is unable to bear the suffering of others is born in you, along with a wish to actually drop whatever you are doing to free another from their predicament. Imagine, for example, that a child has fallen into a pit of fire. His mother wouldn't be able to bear his suffering; she would drop everything and rush to do whatever is necessary to rescue her child from the flames. Drom, it is all very well to think of and love others as your own children, but unless you constantly hold them dear, you'll give other activities a priority. If, however, you have a compassion that is unable to bear the suffering of all, you will easily be able to put aside whatever you are doing and work solely for their benefit.

"Based upon such compassion, you must recognize all beings as having had the experience of being parents to you. The recognition should be a happy one, authentic and free of all partiality. This is what it means to continually be within an experience of joy. Moreover, if buddhahood is won, all happiness and the well-being of both self and others are incidental—as such focus solely on awakening.

"Drom, this is the dawning of great compassion, which views all beings as parents.

"To dedicate love is to meditate on joy—to be joyous at the happiness of others and buddhahood.

"To dedicate joy is to view all without the slightest partiality or bias, to equate your own comfort with that of others, and to induce a nonconceptual wisdom that views all within a great all-pervasive equanimity.

"Drom, the root of altruism is compassion. And in dependence upon this compassion, all the bodhisattvas' dharmas come to be.""

## THE FAULTS OF IGNORING COMPASSION

"Saraha said:

> If your practice of emptiness is devoid of compassion, you have not found the supreme path.

*The Chapter on the Miracles of Manjushri* reads:

> If your understanding of emptiness is one that isn't concerned with others, know it to be the devil's work.

The protector of beings Tsangpa Gyare said:

> A claim to work for the benefit of others that is without compassion is about as much use as dog's meat."

## HOW TO ACTUALLY DEVELOP COMPASSION

"Suppose you now wonder, how should I meditate on such compassion? Well, the person who has shown you the greatest kindness in this life is your mother; as such, this is the initial meditation. *The Mind Training Compendium of Excellent Sayings* reads:

> My mother looks at me with eyes full of compassion; she shows me deep affection, thinks only of my welfare, and protects me from all discomfort and harm. She is unable to bear any suffering I might have, as can be witnessed through her physical, verbal, and mental actions. She is able to endure anything for me; no pain or discomfort is too great.

Think along such lines as these, and give rise to and meditate upon a powerful compassion.

"At times such at these, it is useful to supplicate the guru and the three jewels; it is very easy to give rise to a sense of refuge and very efficacious to take refuge at this point.

"When taking refuge, rest in the equality of self and other, bring your mother to mind, and reflect upon the negative deeds she has unknowingly committed and her suffering.

"Take refuge in the guru and the three jewels from the very core of your being and pledge to refrain from harming others; recite the related verses of refuge, and so on, clearly and loudly.

"Spontaneous experiences of compassion will arise and should be nurtured, but you must know these to be temporary and difficult to hold on to, so continually meditate upon compassion for long periods of time.

"When compassion arises, you will have thoughts of wishing to eradicate your mother's sin and suffering, of wishing to place her in comfort and virtue. You should now reflect that you do not have the ability to place your mother in such states but that the three jewels do have such an ability.

"Reflect that a mother with a crippled hand watching her child being carried away by a river would cry out to another to help rescue him. Supplicate and take refuge in the three jewels with a similar fervor.

"I have used the example of a mother, but it is perfectly acceptable to use your father, or any other person who has shown you exceptional kindness and to whom you feel exceptionally close."

## A MEDITATION ON GREAT SUFFERING

"Reflect on the suffering endured in the realms of hell, spirits, and animals and how you wouldn't be able to endure so much as a fraction of it.

"Similarly, reflect well upon the different types of suffering experienced by children and, more importantly, how your mother tried her best to protect you from them all.

"Think: If I were tormented by the slightest heat, my mother would try to cool me. She would tenderly blow on my food to cool it, before putting it into my mouth. If she thought me cold, she would warm me up. As a baby I was unable to fend for myself; if I was hungry or thirsty she would feed me her milk and give me everything she had without holding anything back. And, should she think me ill or in mortal danger, she would suffer greatly.

"Reflect with compassion, how all your mother/parent sentient beings are experiencing these sufferings of heat, cold, hunger, thirst, stupidity, and dumbness right now. Meditate strongly until compassion arises, after it has arisen reflect how you might eradicate these sufferings and place all your mother beings in bliss. Use the same supplications as before.

"Apply these techniques to those with great suffering—of enemies, sickness, affliction by spirits, financial worry and anxiety over loans, and so on."

## How to Meditate upon Compassion for Negative Persons

"Consider powerful, wealthy, and haughty persons, who, along with their retinues of attendants and servants, create so much negativity in the world. When they pass, they will have no other place to go other than the lower realms. Pondering this should give rise to an extraordinarily strong compassion. If it doesn't, it is said to be a sure sign that in the deep recesses of your mind you still harbor a wish to obtain the enjoyments of the world.

"Persons of such wealth and influence are in a wondrous position to bring about the welfare of both themselves and others; nevertheless, they would rather engage in negative acts in return for a slight benefit—wasting a most beneficial opportunity.

"Bringing about the ruin of their long-term plans for happiness, they are like someone who knowingly drinks poison.

"Reflect upon these points until you are unable to bear them and thereby give rise to a fierce compassion."

## Those Whom It Is Difficult to Develop Compassion Toward

"The most difficult form of this meditation is to focus on a person whom you have benefited greatly and who has returned your kindness by giving you great hardship: Reflect that since time without beginning they have experienced immeasurable suffering, and now, once again, through negative action, such as harming you, and so forth, they are once again gathering causes that will ripen into suffering. Reflect that this is someone who, like all others, has had the experience of being a parent to you countless times and who has shown you great kindness. Reflect on their kindness and meditate as before."

## A REFLECTION UPON ALL SENTIENT BEINGS

"Bring to mind your mother of this life. Now picture her possessed by spirits and driven insane, blind and without a guide, wandering in dangerous places where with every step there is a great danger of stumbling and falling into terrible abysses. Imagine your kind mother is in such a predicament and give rise to an uncontrived, genuine compassion.

"Reflect that all beings have had the experience of being a mother to you and how since time without beginning, they have been insane, possessed and driven insane by the evil spirit of the destructive emotions, their wisdom eye blinded by ignorance, bereft of the guidance of a spiritual friend, wandering along the uneven and dangerous road of samsara, ever close to the edge and a fall ever downward to the three great abysses of the lower realms."

## MEDITATE AND GIVE RISE TO COMPASSION

"It is said that the possession of great merit makes the development of compassion that much easier. In *The Book of Kadam*, Dromtonpa requests from Atisha a meditation upon compassion. He replies:

> Take a good look at sentient beings. They have all taken up a body that is the cause of illness. Now imagine their being stricken with a disease such as leprosy, covered in great sores, conjoined with the ever-increasing pain as the disease takes it toll—there is nothing but distress! How sad! Reflect that each of these beings has at one time or another throughout your many lives had the experience of being a parent to you. Develop strong compassion for them, as nothing other than this is of any use.
>
> Reflect and meditate on the unendurable compassion you'd feel if you witnessed your mother of this life fall into a pit of fire. Similarly, reflect on her being impoverished, destitute, without food, water or clothing. Repeated contemplation will give rise to compassion.
>
> When alone contemplate the sufferings of samsara—such as those experienced by hungry spirits, in the various hell realms and so on. Meditate upon an all-pervasive love—one that cannot bear the suffering of others.

"The meditation technique given in *The Swift Path* is to initially reflect upon the suffering endured by a sheep as she is led before a butcher. Use this image to meditate upon the suffering created and endured by all pitiful beings.

"Clearly imagine a sheep, with her legs tied, lying helplessly on the ground as a butcher opens her chest with his knife, how he plunges his hand inside, his eyes rolling upward as he rummages around to find his mark, the veins of her heart. In a moment, he literally tears away her life."

## CONTEMPLATE THESE SUFFERINGS AND REFLECT

"How wonderful it would be if all beings were free of suffering and the causes of suffering; may they come to be free of them! I will cause them to be free of them! Gurus and deities, pray bless me with the ability to do this.

"To aid in the development of the experience, reflect that the sangha misuse offerings, people live immorally, give up the Dharma, or harbor strange and wrong views. Reflect that they easily harm others and engage in all kinds of negative actions. Bring these and other images to mind and use them to develop your meditation on compassion.

"These, however, are but a few examples of suffering. To elaborate, contemplate the eightfold, sixfold, and threefold sufferings of samsara or, in particular, reflect upon the suffering inherent in each of the six realms. *The Bodhisattva Grounds* says:

> If you have the stomach for it, look with compassion at the 110 types of suffering taught by Buddha, and meditate upon them.

"If, having tried all these different meditation techniques, you still find it difficult to develop compassion, use the methods given in the *Meditation Guide Book to the Heart of Dependent Arising*:

> Having gone for refuge, visualize a seat of a lotus and moon cushion at the crown of your head and meditate on your guru Avalokiteshvara seated upon it. Visualize your mother of this lifetime in front of yourself and recollect the kindness she has shown to you, from the moment of your conception and continually for the entirety of your life. Allow these strong, emotional recollections of her kindness to flood your entire being such that

you cry out, "Oh, my mother!" again and again! Meditate until you feel the hairs on your body begin to move and tears stream from your eyes.

Should this not happen, adopt the following posture of anguish and redouble your efforts at meditation: Sit in a squatting posture, with your knees drawn up to your chest and allow you head to hang down in a gesture of despair. Rest your chin in your palms and place your ring fingers in your mouth. And, just as you might shout out to a friend for help, cry out to your master, "Precious guru, my father, pray guide all sentient beings, my kind mothers, right this very minute along the path to liberation!"

Begin the meditation as above and continue to include all parent beings of the six realms. Contemplate the sufferings of death and change inherent in the realms of the gods; of quarrel and strife in the realms of the titans; as you know, of birth, aging, sickness, and death in the realm of humans; of subservience and being butchered in the animal realm; of hunger and thirst in the realms of hungry ghosts; of boiling and burning in the hot hells and frozen in the cold hells.

Bring their sufferings to mind, give rise to compassion, and with a strong and single-pointedness of mind, recite "Precious guru, my father, pray guide all sentient beings, my kind mothers, right this very minute along the path to liberation!" as before.

Thereafter give rise to an attitude that is able to endure taking the sufferings of all parent beings of the six realms—your old mothers all.

Finally equalize yourself with all others and then meditate— rest in a space-like equipoise, beyond all elaboration.

"Until you have actually given rise to great compassion, it is important to understand that in addition to the meditation session itself, activities outside of the formal sitting practice should be approached mindfully, the continuity of which will serve to enhance your development of compassion. The *Middle-Length Stages of Meditation* says:

Practice compassion while meditating, and similarly when engaging in activities, continually meditate upon compassion for all.

During your postmeditation sessions, continually read the teachings of Buddha on compassion as well as their commentaries. Give them a melody and recite them out loud. *The Book of Kadam* says:

> Drom said, "The enemy, delusion, has taken my parent sentient beings away, and the four great rivers of birth, aging, sickness, and death have carried them far away. The boat to liberation is the supreme guru, directed from the helm and moved with the oars of beneficial deeds, and he sails to bleak and barren shores to rescue these parent beings of mine.
>
> "Lama, like the wish-fulfilling gem of the mighty naga king, pray rescue these parents of mine; with your marvelous brilliance, power, and mastery, guide them, I pray!"

*The Meaning of Enlightened Mind—The Three Kayas* says:

> Throughout the six realms, there isn't a single sentient being who hasn't been a parent to me; sad indeed, that these parents of mine now wander aimlessly in samsara! With the love and concern of a mother at the passing of her only child, take the pledge to liberate all from oceanic samsara.
>
> Just as a mother hen incubates her eggs, give rise to the warmth of love and concern that would establish all in omniscience. Just as the masses wholeheartedly rejoice at the news of a birth in the royal family, give rise to a similar delight and experience a veritable ocean of joy and pleasure. Just as a poor rishi dedicates a torma to a king, be free of ideas of near and far, enemies and friend, and abide in perfect equanimity. And pledge, I will accomplish the unsurpassable Mahayana to place all beings in the highest ground, buddhahood. Should any seek to harm me, I pledge to repay their malevolence with kindness.

"Recite these and any other quotations you may know aloud and contemplate their meaning."

## THE MEASURE OF HAVING MEDITATED UPON COMPASSION

"*The First Stages of Meditation* says:

> When you spontaneously feel compassion, just like a mother feels at the distress of her child, and want to completely alleviate the suffering of all beings, your compassion is complete and can be called great.

Similarly the lordly and most precious master Tsongkhapa says:

> When you spontaneously feel and give rise to a compassion for all beings commensurate with a mother's compassion for her dear and much-loved child, you have perfected great compassion."[4]

I summarized:

> You who never gave up on the awakening of beings,
> And held them all in your love, greatly compassionate Buddha,
> I supplicate you—pray gaze upon all beings, my parents, with
>     compassion.

> You who view a bloodthirsty enemy with the discrimination of their
>     once having been a kind parent and with an extraordinarily strong
>     love,
> Bodhisattvas all—pray guard all beings, my parents, as your children.

> You who saw the misery of beings and didn't remain unmoved,
> Root and lineage gurus who work for the benefit of all—
> Pray pacify the sufferings of each and every sentient being, my
>     parents all.

> In the multitude of my limitless past lives, there isn't a single being
>     who hasn't been a parent to me.
> Sad indeed, those kind parent sentient beings now experience such
>     unwanted suffering.

In past lives, when a brat such as I was hot, my kind parents tried to
cool me.
Sad indeed, that some of those kind parents are now born in the
eight hot hells and experience the extreme suffering of heat!

In past lives, when a brat such as I was cold, my kind parents tried to
warm me.
Sad indeed, that some of those kind parents are now born in the
eight cold hells and experience the extreme suffering of cold!

In past lives, when a brat such as I was hungry or thirsty, my kind
parents gave me food and drink.
Sad indeed, that some of those kind parents are now born as hungry
spirits and experience the extreme suffering of hunger and thirst!

In past lives, when a brat such as I was confused, my kind parents
taught me what to do and what to avoid.
Sad indeed, that some of those kind parents are now born as
animals and experience the extreme sufferings of servitude and
exploitation!

In past lives, when a brat such as I was ill, my kind parents nursed
me.
Sad indeed, that some of those kind parents are now born as humans
and experience the extreme sufferings of illness and death!

In past lives, when a brat such as I was scared, my kind parents
comforted me.
Sad indeed, that some of those kind parents are now born as titans
and experience the extreme sufferings of quarrel and strife!

In past lives, when a brat such as I was lacking something, my kind
parents filled my heart's desires.
Sad indeed, that some of those kind parents are now born as gods
and experience the extreme sufferings of death and the fall!

Kye-hu! How sad!! There is no being who hasn't been a parent to me
and there is no happiness in samsara.

Yet I haven't the slightest ability to protect anyone!
Kye-ma Kye-hu! How terribly sad!!

Such is the state of things!
Parent sentient beings afflicted by hundreds of sufferings, and bereft
    of the slightest comfort.
How wonderful if all beings were free of suffering and the causes of
    suffering; may they come to be free of them!

In this and throughout all my past lives, sentient beings have all, at
    one time or another, been a kind parent to me.
I will take away their suffering and place them all in bliss—
Gurus, bless me to accomplish this!

Through the force of the merit I have accumulated throughout the
    three times,
May the sufferings of heat, cold, hunger, thirst, servitude, sickness,
    death, strife, passing away, and the fall from heaven,
Along with all the other sufferings experienced within the six realms
    be thoroughly pacified.

In this and throughout all lives to come, may I never be parted from
    the most precious mind of compassion—supreme ornament
    of all Dharma practitioners, wish-fulfilling gem—source of
    innumerable qualities and root of all Dharma practice.

Recite these words while reflecting deeply upon their meaning and before
too long you will easily give rise to great compassion. To be able to fulfill the
wishes of both yourself and all others it is imperative to apply great effort at
the practice of meditation!

# 9

# Nurturing Love and Compassion

*The Eight Thoughts of a Great and Noble Being*

---

My fortunate student, the devoted, generous, and highly intelligent Lhaje Kunga, offered me many precious things, such as turquoises to ornament the ears, and so on, and, along with various acts of devotion, asked me to teach him an instruction that would definitely lead him to buddhahood. After making his request, he sang:

> Lordly yogi, like a book of scripture—
> Upon the dark paper of your brilliant mind,
> The vast and profound Dharma is written in gold,
> And it is wrapped in the *dharani* cover of unforgetfulness.

> Lordly yogi, like a sword—
> The double-edged blade of your wisdom is incredibly sharp;
> See how it slashes the net of confusion—
> Ignorance, misunderstanding, and doubt.

> I prostrate and make offering to you.
> I confess my failings and misdeeds in their entirety,
> Rejoice in virtue, and request from you the vast and profound
>     dharmas.
> Please remain, I supplicate, and to this end I dedicate all accumulated
>     virtue;
> Pray remain for hundreds of aeons!

> Perfect and most precious guru,
> You are the keeper of the precious treasury—
> The instructions of the profound view and extensive conduct—
> In your great kindness, please pay me heed.

I was once under the influences of this life's affairs,
And squandered my precious life of freedom and endowment in
    frivolous worldly activity.

Now the chance to practice is almost up for I am old and about to
    die;
The impermanence of things moves me ever closer to death and I feel
    sad.

However, having come into your presence, O guru—
Reverent and most precious master—
Please teach me something that will be useful at the time of death
    and bless me with the ability to put it into practice.

From now on, and in all my future lives, may I never be separate from
    you;
And by receiving, contemplating, and meditating upon your
    instructions, just as you've taught them,
May I swiftly achieve the state of Buddha.

In reply I taught him the following: If you want to become Buddha, you must enter through the greater vehicle gateway of the sutras and tantras, and practice one pure dharma exceptionally well. The dharma of which I speak is the very foundation of the greater vehicle—it is the practice of love and compassion. In addition, if you contemplate the eight thoughts of great beings, you'll perfect the vast accumulation of merit and without too much difficulty, you'll become enlightened. The wise ones all agree it's important to practice in this way, and if you are wondering how to begin, consider how all beings have at some time during the infinity of your past lives acted as your kind mother, father, friends, and relatives. They have in this capacity offered you immeasurable benefits and protected you from countless harms. At this very time, leaving aside the everlasting bliss and happiness of uncontaminated liberation, the state of omniscience, they are even bereft of contaminated bliss, the temporal prosperity of gods and humans—such as that enjoyed by Brahma, Indra, and so forth. Thereby cultivate compassion for them. Recite as follows: "How wonderful it would be, if all my kind parent sentient beings could enjoy both contaminated and uncontaminated bliss, and their cause—virtue. May they come to have them; I will cause this myself! Gurus and deities, pray bless me with the ability to do this!" Along with this contemplation, meditate for long periods upon a fierce love that encompasses all beings.

Contemplate the dissatisfactory nature of samsara in general: birth, aging, sickness, death, possession, abject poverty, meeting, separation, squabbles, fights, and so forth. Moreover, consider the specific sufferings: the heat and cold of the hells, the hunger and thirst of the hungry spirits, and the exploitation of animals. Give rise to an intense compassion for all beings experiencing them. Recite as follows: "How wonderful it would be, if all my kind parent sentient beings could be free of the dissatisfactory nature of samsara, in general, and of the three lower realms, in particular. May they come to be free of them. I will cause this myself. Gurus and deities, pray bless me with the ability to do this!" Along with this contemplation meditate earnestly, time and time again, upon a fierce compassion for all beings.

Additionally contemplate the following:

1. I have the power to remove the suffering of all beings who have at one time or another been my kind parents.
2. I have the capacity to grant great wealth to those suffering from poverty.
3. I can offer my flesh and blood for the benefit of others.
4. I'm able to remain in hell for long periods for the sake of beings.
5. I'm able to use the wealth of the world and of that there beyond to fulfill the wishes of sentient beings.
6. After becoming Buddha, I'll definitely work to remove the suffering of all beings.
7. In this and throughout all my future lives, I'll give up that which is of no use to others; solely enjoying the taste of the ultimate; words that are not pleasing to others; feelings that are not altruistic; delighting in the pain of others; and an obsession with my body, wisdom, wealth, and power.
8. May the effects of the negative actions of others ripen upon me, and may the results of my positive actions ripen upon them.

These are the eight thoughts of exceptional beings. They may just be thoughts, but they are spectacular! If the great beings of the past have told us how they meditated upon them, is there any need to mention how we need to do likewise? Therefore meditate with great diligence!

I supplicate at the feet of my kind masters,
Pray bless me to give rise to love and compassion!

Alas!
There are no beings that haven't had the experience of being my
    parents,
And there is not a moment's pleasure in samsara.
May I lovingly hold those bereft of bliss,
And be compassionate to those weary with suffering.

Considering that I have the power to remove this unwanted suffering,
And, when appropriate, to grant great wealth to those suffering from
    poverty,
To offer my actual body, my flesh, blood, and bones for the benefit of
    others,
To remain in hell for long periods to greatly benefit beings,
To use great wealth to fulfill the wishes of sentient beings,
After becoming Buddha, I'll definitely remove the suffering of
    beings.
In this and throughout all my future lives,
I'll give up that which is of no use to others,
Solely enjoying the taste of the ultimate,
Words that are not pleasing to others,
Feelings that are not altruistic,
An obsession with my body, wisdom, wealth, and power, and
    delighting in the pain of others.

Finally, may the effects of the negative actions of others ripen upon
    me,
And may the results of my positive actions ripen upon them.

Precious and most glorious root guru,
Pray bless me to train in altruism!

If you recite these words while contemplating their meaning, the experiences of love, compassion, and the altruistic wish to benefit others—bodhichitta—will effortlessly arise one after the other. You'll enter the ranks of
the greater vehicle, and become an irreversible bodhisattva.

# The Cultivation of Bodhichitta

My fortunate disciple, the naturally kind-hearted and ethically pure Lobsang Dundrup, told me of his need for a complete, clear, and concise explanation of the methods for developing bodhichitta: the mind trainings of the seven-point cause and effect as well as the equalizing and exchange of self and others as found in *The Great Treatise on the Stages of the Path to Enlightenment*—the most regal, jewellike instruction, which never fails to fulfill the wishes of all beings without exception. He sang:

Spiritual friend who views all beings as his mother—
Countless aeons ago you continually gave rise to the supreme mind
of bodhichitta for the benefit of us all.

Seeing self-cherishing as the door to suffering and cherishing others
as the basis of all qualities,
You abandoned the former,
And with great delight, you took up the latter.

Dissatisfaction comes from wanting happiness for oneself alone,
Whereas bliss comes from altruism.
Having perfectly understood this distinction, you exchanged your
happiness for the misery of others.

Aroused by great compassion, you tirelessly work for the welfare of
others.
And to your enemies—those longing to harm you—
You show an even greater love,
And go out of your way to try to help them.

By churning the milk-like Dharma, the butter of bodhichitta is
  produced;
Even though I know this to be true,
I'm still unable to disentangle myself.

Therefore, O guru, having mastered the techniques of exchanging
  self and other,
You really are meaningful to behold!

I offer you homage and make the following request:

Kindly teach me the profound pith instructions for developing
  bodhichitta:
Those of the seven-point cause and effect,
And the equalizing and exchange of self and others in accordance
  with the regal, jewellike instruction—
The *Great Exposition of the Stages of the Path to Enlightenment*—
Of the victor Lobsang Drakpa, Manjushri in the guise of a man.

I replied, "Let's begin with the seven-point cause and effect mind training
technique for developing bodhichitta:

1. Recognizing all beings as having been your mother: Consider the
   infinity of your previous lives, during which there isn't a single
   being who hasn't had the experience of being your mother. Furthermore, the omniscient Buddha has mentioned how all beings
   have been one's parents innumerable times. Consider these statements with the utmost care, and you'll come to the conclusion that
   there isn't a single being who hasn't had the experience of being a
   kind mother to you.
2. Recalling their kindness: All beings have, in turn, had the experience of having been your mother; for example, bring to mind your
   mother of this life. Recall how she took care of you, affording you
   immeasurable care and protecting you from countless harms. In
   short, all beings have shown you nothing but kindness.
3. Wishing to repay that kindness: To take a worldly example, if
   someone were shown a kindness, let's say someone gave them
   food or clothing, or saved them from a difficult situation. To not

repay this kindness would lose them the respect of society at large, wouldn't it? Similarly, if we consider the care and protection our kind mothers have shown us time and time again, since time without beginning, should we not wish to repay it, disdain alone will be our lot, wouldn't it? In this way, give rise to a fine attitude and think: 'I will do whatever I can to repay the kindness shown to me by all mother sentient beings.'

4. Love: All beings wish to be happy and avoid suffering. However, their aspirations and actions are in conflict with one another, and they engage only in the causes of further dissatisfaction. Leaving aside temporary liberation, consider the most powerful gods of the higher realms, Brahma and Indra, or, among humans, the universal monarch, none of them enjoy happiness. Leaving them aside, consider most humans: there is no real happiness in even the most affluent of houses. In addition, consider the plight of those in the three lower realms of existence, those who have exhausted all options and experience nothing but suffering. How wonderful if all of them, my mothers, were to be happy. May it come to pass, and, just as in the example of a loving mother who relieves the sadness of her child by giving him food and clothing, may I cause all beings to be happy. In this way, meditate upon a heart-warming love toward all.

5. Compassion: Besides sentient beings' general lack of happiness, there are inconceivable sufferings to be reflected upon. Consider the heat and cold endured in the hells, the hunger and thirst experienced by spirits, the sufferings of servitude and exploitation endured by animals. Think of the human situation: having to look after all that one possesses, the desperate search for something one doesn't have and the disappointment of not getting it, the suffering of meeting with enemies and unpleasant situations, as well as separation from pleasant circumstances and friends, and of course, the more usual sufferings of birth, aging, sickness, and death. Think of the demigods and their sufferings of conflict and strife, and also of the gods with their suffering of death and subsequent fall from the divine. How wonderful if all my mother beings who endure such terrible sufferings were to be free of them. May they be free of suffering, and, just as in the example of a mother whose compassion will not allow her to stand by and see her only child

fall into a fire, may I have an equal compassion toward all. In this way, meditate upon great compassion.

6. Supreme intention: Within a fierce love and compassion for all beings, think as follows: 'All beings—my destitute mothers—are bereft of happiness and tormented by uninterrupted sufferings. If they cannot rely upon me, their child, to help them, upon whom can they rely? If I cannot benefit them, who will?' Reflecting thus, think as follows: 'I will free all mother beings from this continual suffering—the torments of samsara in general, and of the three lower realms in particular. I alone will place those deprived of happiness in the temporary happiness of the god and human realms, and ultimately I shall lead them all to the state of permanent bliss—the liberation of the omniscient one, Buddha.' With this, meditate perfectly upon the supreme intention.

7. Bodhichitta: You may well have the resolve to free all beings from their sufferings and place them in the state of happiness, but, for the time being at least, leaving aside the notion of all beings, you do not even have the means to remove a single suffering, destructive emotion, or karmic tendency; you do not even know where you are headed. Who then, you should wonder, has such an ability? The complete and perfect Buddha, having exhausted all faults and possessed of all qualities, does. If you could achieve such a state, a single shaft of light from your radiant body would have the potential, in a single instant, to clear away the sufferings of billions of beings and place them all in a state of happiness. Therefore think: 'For the sake of both myself and all others, it is imperative that I achieve the state of buddhahood. How wonderful if I could achieve it so very quickly. I will do so! I will do whatever it takes to achieve it right away!' Train your mind accordingly.

"As to training your mind in the equalizing and exchange of self and others, once you have given rise to the strong wish to quickly become a perfect Buddha, you may wonder, now what? Previously, when the Buddha was a bodhisattva on the path of training, he had a strong resolve to become enlightened for the benefit of all mother beings. All notions of self-interest faded, and he cherished others dearly; continually he took loss and defeat upon himself and gave away all gain and victory to others. Finally, he became Buddha.

"We, on the other hand, don't have the slightest concern for others and have only our own selfish interests at heart. With this attitude, not only will we fail to achieve our aims, but up until now this attitude has only caused us to wander in samsara and experience suffering!

"Thinking that you'll follow in the footsteps of the Buddha, give rise to the thought: 'How wonderful it would be if, for the sake of all sentient beings, I were to cherish others more than myself—to take loss and defeat upon myself and offer all gain and victory to others—in order to achieve buddhahood as quickly as possible; I will do it!'

"The thought, 'I will do whatever it takes,' is the supreme mind training, and if you train in these points, you'll swiftly become enlightened." I sang:

I supplicate my kind masters, pray bless me to develop bodhichitta!

Just as the sky is vast, so is the number of sentient beings,
And each of them without exception has at one time or another been
    a parent to me.
Although appearances have changed, their kindness still remains—
Similar, as it is, to the kindness shown to me by the parents of this
    life.
Kind parents, how I need to repay the kindness you showed me!

Love those without happiness,
And be compassionate to the wretched, who are suffering so.

Think: I will remove the suffering of all beings,
And place them all in the enduring bliss of buddhahood—
To this end, I will endeavor to achieve the state of the perfect Buddha.

Just as Prince Siddhartha, by giving up self-interest and focusing on
    the needs of others, became Buddha,
Similarly, I too will give up self-interest and work at the welfare of
    others.

When he was the Prince Vishvantara, he gave away his children and
    realm.
Similarly, I too, without any sense of reservation, should give away
    the wealth and companions held so dear.

When he was Prince Mahamaitribala, he nourished a tigress with his own flesh.
Similarly, I too should joyfully give this cherished heap of an illusory body to the hordes of flesh-eaters.

When he was King Maitribala, he nourished harmful demons with his own blood.
Similarly, I too should lovingly give the warm blood of my heart, so difficult to part with, to the blood-drinkers.

When he was the merchant's son Jalavahana, he saved fish by reciting the name of the Tathagata.
Similarly, I too should give the sacred Dharma to all beings who lack it.

When he was Prince Mahakalyanartha, he compassionately endured prince Papartha's ingratitude.
Similarly, I too should have great compassion toward my companion's ingratitude, stirred up as it is by negative dispositions.

When he was the bodhisattva monkey, he pulled a wicked man out of a well.
Similarly, I too should guide evil people compassionately, without expecting anything in return, even if it is to my detriment.[1]

May this merit, and all merit gathered over the three times,
Serve as the cause for us all to perfect supreme bodhichitta,
And, until we reach enlightenment,
May we never be separated from bodhisattvas.

Recite these words aloud and pause to contemplate their meaning.

If you train your mind in these instructions, the qualities of love, compassion, and the precious mind of bodhichitta will naturally come to arise in you.

# II

# ON TAKING THE BODHISATTVA'S VOW

*The Four Black and Four White Deeds*

---

My faithful, eager, and compassionate student Jinpa Sangye presented me a measure of tsampa, together with a celestial scarf. He asked for instruction:

> In the example set by the incomparable Buddha,
> Initially he gave rise to bodhichitta,
> And strove for many aeons to amass the collections of merit and wisdom,
> Which culminated in his achievement of perfect buddhahood.
>
> I pay homage to you, O ornament of our crowns,
> And respectfully make to you this request:
>
> I, a Dharma-less monk, a hoarder of gifts,
> Was, initially, very confused.
> I then gave rise to the five poisons,
> Which culminated in the accumulating of much negative karma,
> And now you find me like this, bereft of the Dharma.
>
> Precious master, getting to know you has caused me to think much about the sublime Dharma;
> Pray grant me an instruction both vast and profound of the means to achieve buddhahood.
>
> From now until my enlightenment,
> I request that you continually care for me,
> And through your compassion,
> May I practice the sublime Dharma well,
> And swiftly attain buddhahood!

In reply I gave him the following teaching: Our compassionate teacher initially gave rise to the excellent thought of bodhichitta. He then strove for three countless great aeons to perfect the accumulations, which culminated in his perfect realization of buddhahood. For us, his followers, giving rise to the thought of bodhichitta is extremely important.

Should you wonder how this should be done: In the presence of your guru and representations of enlightened body, speech, and mind, or by visualizing them and having the conviction that your guru, the Buddha, along with the other deities of the merit field are seated amid brilliant lights and rainbows in the space before you, vividly clear and radiant, offer them the seven-limbed homage, present a mandala, and turn to them for refuge.

To actually take the bodhichitta vow, think: "For the sake of all parent sentient beings, I must achieve the state of buddhahood. To this end, I will engage in the bodhisattva's activities, such as the six perfect actions, and so forth." And then recite the following three times:

> All you buddhas and bodhisattvas pray pay me heed!
> Just as the buddhas of the past gave rise to bodhichitta and trained
>     in stages in the precepts of the bodhisattvas,
> So now do I, for the benefit of beings, give rise to bodhichitta,
> And vow to train in stages in the precepts of the bodhisattvas.[1]

And rejoice while reciting:

> Today my life has borne fruit;
> I have used it well,
> To have become of the Buddha's lineage, his child and heir.
>
> In every way, then, I shall undertake activities befitting such a
>     position,
> And will do nothing that would sully this high and faultless lineage.

To protect your bodhichitta from deteriorating, you must abandon the four black actions:

1. Lying and deceiving one's guru, abbot, master, and so on
2. Causing others to regret the virtuous actions they've done
3. Getting angry with and speaking unpleasantly to bodhisattvas
4. In an absence of sincerity, using deceit and pretense

And to cause its increase, take up the following four white actions:

1. Never lying to anyone, even in jest or as a joke
2. Being honest, never a deceiver
3. Praising bodhisattvas
4. Causing those who rely on you spiritually to avoid the limited vehicle and embrace the path leading to perfect buddhahood

In addition, you should also perfect the two accumulations by making offerings to the three jewels, and so on. I sang:

> I supplicate my kind guru; pray bless me to train in the supreme mind of bodhichitta.

> Just as the teacher, the Buddha, first gave rise to bodhichitta,
> Similarly, I too will bring forth the awakened mind as intention and engagement.
> Either in front of my guru, or while visualizing him in the space in front of me,
> I shall offer the seven branches and a mandala,
> And go for refuge.

> All buddhas and bodhisattvas dwelling in the buddha fields of the ten directions, pray pay me heed!

> Just as the past sugatas initially gave rise to bodhichitta and serially trained in the bodhisattva deeds,
> I will also give rise to the awakened mind,
> And will serially train in the bodhisattva deeds.

> As the result of past merit, I possess a precious human life of freedom and endowment,
> And today I have taken birth in the Buddha's lineage.
> I have become the perfect Buddha's heir.

> From henceforth I shall abide well within this well-respected and pure lineage,
> And only undertake action that accords with it.

I shall give up the four black actions that cause bodhichitta to
   decline:
Lying to and deceiving my guru, abbot, and master,
Causing regret for virtue undertaken,
Getting angry with and speaking unpleasantly to bodhisattvas,
And being insincere—using deceit and pretense,

And take up the four white actions, the cause of its increase:
Never lying, even in jest,
Being honest, never a deceiver,
Praising bodhisattvas,
And, encouraging those requesting guidance to enter the gateway of
   the greater vehicle.

Moreover, for the increase of the awakening mind,
I shall make effort to amass the two collections.
Precious and most glorious root guru,
Pray bless me to train in the supreme bodhichitta.

May the merit arising here—as well as any gathered over the three
   times—
serve as a cause for the proliferation of the awakened mind.
In this and in all future lives, may I never be separated from it!

In this way continually develop bodhichitta.

# THE BODHISATTVA'S VOW

*The Six Perfections and the Four Means of Gathering Disciples*

One day my worthy disciple Lobsang Gelek, one with great respect for his teachers, love for his Dharma friends, and compassion for all beings, came to visit, bringing me many provisions. He respectfully bowed and asked for instruction with the following verses:

> Having given rise to the excellent bodhichitta,
> Your enlightened attitude is to exchange yourself with others.

> With no attachment to your possessions, you offer them as charity,
> And you protect your morality as you do your eyes.
> You meditate upon patience, even if it were to cost you your life,
> And with effort, you accumulate merit for others' benefit.
> Remaining within an unmoving samadhi, you are omniscient—
> knowing both appearance and its nature.

> Master of means, you work for others through the four means of
> gathering disciples and have completed the dual benefit of self and
> others!

> Precious and glorious master,
> I prostrate at your feet and make offerings.
> Kindly give heed to this stupid disciple's request.

> Time and time again I have heard of how the bodhisattva,
> After giving rise to bodhichitta—both as an aspiration and as an
> engagement—
> Matures his mind by accumulating the collections of merit and
> wisdom,

And matures the minds of others by training in the altruistic means
    of the fourfold method of gathering disciples—
Yet still I don't understand.

Pray teach me, in accord with the instructions of the masters of old,
    such as the great and omniscient pandit,
In a way that is short, concise, and clear,
Exactly how the bodhisattvas of the great vehicle accomplish their
    own aims as well as those of others

From now and in all of my future lives, may I please only you,
And by practicing your instruction—both vast and profound—
May I swiftly become enlightened.

    I replied, "Having given rise to sublime bodhichitta, mature you own
mind with the six perfect actions:

1. The practice of charity: Without any thought for fame or personal
   gain, teach as much Dharma as you can to those who are impoverished of and desirous to hear it. This constitutes the giving of
   Dharma.
       Protect those tormented by violent humans, nonhuman enti-
   ties, elemental spirits, and so forth. This is the gift of placing them
   out of harm's way, the giving of fearlessness.
       Teach the poverty-stricken and destitute not to simply hope for
   wealth but how to actively abandon the cause of poverty—miser-
   liness. In addition, offering them whatever material aid you can
   constitutes the giving of material things. Practice these three as
   much as you can.
2. The practice of morality: Give up the ten negative actions, and
   refrain from transgressing whatever vows you have taken. Engage
   in and enhance your own ethical and virtuous behavior, as well
   as your practice of the six perfect actions—charity and the rest.
   Introduce others to the pure and virtuous path of ethics, and so
   on, and thereby set them on the spiritual path of maturation and
   liberation.
3. The practice of patience: Should the whole world arise as your
   enemy, if you do not give rise to so much as a moment of anger

in retaliation—repaying harm with benevolence—you have perfected the Buddha's teachings, such as the perfect action of patience, and so forth, benefiting both yourself and others.

Moreover, when bereft of adequate food, finance, dwelling, and so forth, or afflicted by the unwanted sufferings of sudden illness, and so forth, understand these experiences to be none other than the effects of your past negative actions. Thereby, not only are you purifying said karma, which you will not need to endure again, but by practicing the dharma—patiently enduring these situations—you'll progress on your spiritual path to omniscience. If sufferings such as these are accepted and utilized, you can sever the cause for both your and others' rebirth in the cycle of contaminated existence, in general, and the lower realms, in particular.

Also having faith in the ripening of various negative and positive actions, the blessings of the triple gem, the inconceivable power of the mighty buddhas and bodhisattvas, highest enlightenment and the twelve scriptural references,[1] and the main points of the bodhisattva's training delivers a vast result. If you trust in these, you'll definitely come to achieve the highest enlightenment. For the main points of the bodhisattva's training are the subject matter and meaning of the twelve scriptural references, and it is imperative that you put these into practice.

4. The practice of effort: The Buddha's major and minor marks of perfection and the bodhisattva's practice of patience both need to be perfected. A bodhisattva would not give up their practice even if it meant remaining in the hell of continuous torment for hundreds of thousands of aeons; they would endeavor. Similarly, you should never give up the thought to become enlightened, whether you are trying to realize the profound and vast Dharma yourself, or are helping others with their own virtuous practices.

5. The practice of meditation: Essentially meditation is of two types, that which is of the world and that which is beyond it. From the point of view of direction, there are divisions into calm abiding, special insight, and the union of the two. In terms of function, there is meditation that serves to bring physical and mental bliss to your life, meditation that serves as a support for developing qualities, and meditation that brings about the welfare of others. You need to practice them all.

6. The practice of wisdom: An awareness of the natural state is wisdom realizing the ultimate. An understanding of the five sciences is wisdom realizing the conventional.[2] And then there is wisdom as to the best way to aid others. You must practice them all.

"Mature the minds of others by means of the four ways of gathering beings:

1. Generosity: by being generous others will be attracted to you
2. Pleasing speech: teaching in a way that is careful and clear
3. Meaningful conduct: engaging in the practice of the Dharma
4. Practicing what you teach: your practice should be in accord with the practices you teach to others—practice what you preach

"In dependence on these four altruistic points, you will be able to set all beings on the path to maturation and liberation—to buddhahood." I sang:

> I supplicate at the feet of my kind masters,
> Pray bless me to mature and liberate both myself and others
> So as to become Buddha for the benefit of others!

> Having given up the seeking of fame, gain, and the like, I will teach
>     Dharma to those destitute thereof,
> Give freedom from fear to those in danger,
> And be generous to the poor.

> I shall ethically train in an abstinence from misdeeds,
> And actively engage in virtue and altruism.

> Without the slightest aggression, I will endure those who wish me
>     harm,
> Be patient with the difficulties that come along the path,
> And patiently persevere with the practice,
> Until a certainty of the Dharma is won.

> I will don the great armor of a long campaign,
> Engage in efforts to actualize the virtuous dharmas,
> And endeavor to altruistic heights.

I will practice meditation: both of this world and beyond,
Calm abiding, special insight, and their union,
And that which brings both physical and mental bliss.

And I will train in the wisdom realizing the ultimate—an awareness
of the natural state—
In the wisdom realizing the conventional—an understanding of the
five sciences—
And in the wisdom that ascertains the best way to be of service to
others.

To attract disciples, I shall be generous.
Once gathered, I will pleasantly explain the Dharma to them,
Engaging in its practice, may my conduct and the Dharma accord.
By means of these four altruistic points, may I place all beings on the
path that matures and liberates.

Glorious and precious root guru, please bless me with the ability to
accomplish this!

I dedicate the merit gathered over the three times and exemplified
hereby, as a cause for accomplishing the dual purpose of self and
other.

Throughout all my future lives, may I be able to train in these six
perfect actions and four means!

Recite these verses and dwell upon their meaning. If you perform such
a reflective meditation over these key points, the day will surely come
when you'll have the ability to fearlessly engage in the vast deeds of the
bodhisattvas.

# 13

# An Explanation of Langri Thangpa's
## *Eight Verses of Mind Training*

My devoted, generous, and most intelligent disciple Khedrup offered me many precious things, including silver and sheep. He said, "Since I am old and about to die, I need you to grant me a profound instruction that will guarantee my future buddhahood." He sang:

You are the unrivalled root of all that is good,
The single door leading to all excellent paths,
Perfect guide to marvelous places—
The buddha fields of the four kayas—
To your feet, O guru, I offer homage.

I offer you obeisance with my body, speech, and mind, along with a
    practice that will equal my life span.
I openly confess my previous misdeeds,
Engaged in while under the control of this life's affairs,
And rejoice in all, outer, inner, and secret virtue.
I request you to turn the wheel of Dharma for us all,
And beseech you to remain with us and pass not into nirvana.
I dedicate all merit to your ideals, my venerable master!

Root guru, both glorious and precious,
Kindly grant this old man a spiritual instruction,
One that is the essence of the Buddha's teachings—
A sure method for achieving buddhahood that is both concise and
    easy to practice.

Through the compassion of the supreme and incomparable lama,
May I remain undistracted by the myriad affairs of this life,

And, having boarded the boat of hearing, contemplation, and
  meditation,
Set sail for the jewel isle of liberation.

I replied, "If you want to achieve the state of Buddha, you must definitely practice the instructions of the Tibetan master Langri Thangpa Dorje
Sengye. Renowned as an emanation of Buddha Amitabha, Langri Thangpa
was able to gather the meaning of the Buddha's teachings in their entirety.
He then put it into an unprecedented instruction, a veritable wish-fulfilling
jewel, *The Eight Verses of Mind Training*, which is extremely important to
practice.

1. For the moment, let us leave aside all sentient beings that have had
   the experience of being our kind parents in the past, and consider
   just one impoverished individual. If, motivated by bodhichitta, we
   were to give him, say, a meal or an article of clothing, the merit
   ensuing would, in this lifetime, give us the comforts of joy, happiness, and praise. In the future, we would be born into a wealthy
   family and enjoy the infinite delights of humans and gods. Ultimately, it would serve as a cause for our eradicating all faults and
   accumulating all qualities—buddhahood itself.

   Picture an enemy or someone who wishes you harm. If we were
   able, through the fortune of having meditated upon patience, to
   practice patience with them just this once, it would, in the short
   term, greatly increase our store of merit, cause others to praise us
   as a good practitioner, and cause those of the human and divine
   realms to love and care for us. As for the long term, throughout all
   our future births, we will have a fine form and will be able to gather
   a large entourage of respectful disciples. Ultimately, it would serve
   as a cause for the major and minor marks that adorn the form kaya
   of our future buddhahood—at which time we would have become
   the crown ornament of all.

   Therefore, if in reliance upon one or two individuals we can
   fulfill all of our temporary and ultimate wishes, what need is
   there to mention all sentient beings? For this reason, seeing how
   all parent sentient beings are the source of our entire temporary
   and ultimate qualities, they should be viewed as a wish-fulfilling jewel. You should continually cherish each and every one of

them dearly, as you do the eyes in your head or the heart in your chest.

2. In whatever setting you may find yourself, be it pleasant or otherwise, a town, monastic setting, or a hermitage, with whomever you associate, be they monastic or laity, male or female, it is essential to take a lowly position. Seeing all others as a wish-fulfilling jewel, the source of all of our qualities, it is imperative that, without the least regard for their status or position in society, you treat them all respectfully—serving and praising them with the utmost respect, physically, verbally, and mentally.

3. Whether walking, moving about, lying down, or sitting you must continually check your mind. If you find the disturbing emotions, such as attachment or aversion arise, in either strong or subtle ways, you must immediately counter them. Seeing how these destructive states of mind endanger both yourself and those around you, take immediate steps to avert them.

4. Whenever you occasion to meet really nasty people who continually amass great amounts of negative karma, or those oppressed by harsh suffering, don't look away, for you have found a precious treasure! Consider how rare it is to meet someone of their like and hold them especially dear.

5. When others out of jealousy needlessly revile, slander, taunt, and strike you, there is no need to retaliate in kind. Rather, remind yourself that this unpleasant experience is nothing other than the repayment of a previous karmic debt and that you will not have to undergo this particular karmic retribution again. Once certainty is gained, consider that if you do not want to undergo such unpleasant experiences ever again, you must stop engaging in their causes right away. If you do entertain such causes, you can expect further unpleasantness, with trouble, strife, harm, and blame following you wherever you go. Therefore accept the defeat and loss, and proffer the gain and victory to your kind parent sentient beings—the source of your happiness and bliss.

6. When someone you have helped or in whom you have placed great trust, for example, a close relative, a monastic, a friend, a dharma friend, a disciple or patron, either male or female, not only doesn't repay the kindness you've shown them but goes on to take the very food from your mouth, the shirt from your back, the money

from your hands, and so on, this is an extremely nasty and rude individual indeed! However, in this individual, you have found the perfect spiritual friend, someone whose kindness can help you complete the perfect actions of charity and patience!

7. In brief, then, contemplate offering your benefit and joy in its entirety directly and indirectly to all mother beings. In secret, take their pain and sufferings upon yourself—both in actuality and as an aspiration.

8. The above meditations should be kept free and unblemished by the eight worldly concerns: gain and loss, fame and disgrace, slander and praise, pleasure and pain. Understand everything to be illusory and dreamlike, train in detachment, and thereby become free of your former bonds.

"It is said that these eight practices are indispensable for freeing you from your former fetters. The great beings of the past put them into verse and recited them:

1. With the thought to accomplish the highest welfare for all
   sentient beings,
   Who surpass even the wish-fulfilling jewel, may I always hold
   them dear.

2. Whenever I associate with others, I will view myself as the lowest
   among all,
   And from the very depths of my heart, may I hold others as supreme.

3. In all activities, I'll continually check my mind,
   And as soon as disturbing emotions arise,
   Endangering both myself and others,
   May I firmly face and avert them.

4. Whenever I see nasty beings,
   And those oppressed by harsh evil and suffering,
   It is as if finding a precious treasure!
   May I hold them dear as they are seldom met.

5. When others due to jealousy, revile me with abuse, slander, and
   the like, may I accept the loss and offer the victory to them.

6. When one, whom I've helped or in whom I have placed great hope,
   Causes severe harm to me,
   May I view such a one as an excellent spiritual friend.

7. In brief, may I offer, directly and indirectly,
   All benefit and joy to all mother beings.
   And in secret, may I take all their suffering and pain upon
      myself.
8. May I keep all of these practices free from pollution, the defiled
   thought of the eight worldly dharmas, and, understanding all
   phenomena to be illusory, be unattached, free from bondage.

We should also recite these blessed verses, including them in our daily practices. Start practicing them serially right away. In the short term, you'll
accomplish the welfare of both yourself and others and, ultimately, achieve
perfect buddhahood."

# 14

# THE CULTIVATION OF CALM ABIDING

My disciple Thaye Gyatso, an adept in the three higher trainings and two aspects of bodhichitta, asked me for a summary, easy to both understand and practice, of the six causes leading to calm abiding, the eight antidotes to the five hindrances, the nine mental placements, the six powers, and the four mental engagements, all as explained in that excellent book *The Great Treatise on the Stages of the Path to Enlightenment*, a veritable ocean of knowledge fed from the flow of a thousand fine scriptures. He sang:

> In meditation you're immovable, as stable as a mountain,
> When focused, immutably attentive,
> The bliss of pliancy pervades your being,
> And you continually dwell in joy.
>
> Unmistaken and precious lama,
> Kindly grant me a moment.
> With total devotion, I offer homage to you,
> O venerable one, please listen.
>
> I, one whose mind is completely distracted,
> May recite mantras for aeons without effect.
> For the scriptures tell us that to lack calm abiding is to yield the
>     mind to distraction's dictate.
>
> Spiritual seekers writing about this incorrectly have fallen short of
>     the mark,
> And so the most precious of masters,
> The king of the Dharma, Tsongkhapa,
> Wrote the glorious explanation,
> *The Great Treatise on the Stages of the Path to Enlightenment,*

A volume into which all scriptures flow,
Just as all rivers flow to the ocean.

There calm abiding is made easy,
For it explains the causes of its cultivation,
The eight antidotes to the five hindrances,
The nine mental placements, the six powers,
And the four mental engagements.

Through your great love, heed my request—
Please give me a brief outline of these points,
At once both easy to grasp and practice,
And through your compassionate blessings,
May calm abiding, flawless, and rich with pliancy's bliss,
    be born within me.

To which I replied, "Ah yes, to cultivate calm abiding you need six causes:

1. To dwell in a pleasing place with everything favorable and nothing adverse to meditation
2. To have few desires and little concern about resources and clothing
3. To be content with whatever you have, no matter how inferior
4. To abandon activities such as business transactions, astrology, and medicine
5. To perfectly protect the vows and commitments you've taken
6. By contemplating birth, death, and the faults of samsara, to thoroughly give up the concerns of this life

"Know the five hindrances to meditation to be as follows:

1. Laziness—you delight in the distraction that should be absent from your meditation
2. Forgetfulness—when focusing upon an object in meditation, such as the image of the Buddha, you forget the instructions
3. Laxity and excitement—you allow these two to disturb your meditative equipoise
4. Not applying the antidotes when laxity and excitement arise
5. Applying the antidotes when they are no longer needed

"The eight antidotes to these hindrances are as follows. When beset by laziness during meditation

1. recall the qualities of meditation and generate confidence in the practice,
2. develop a yearning to practice meditation,
3. maintain a strong sense of perseverance, and
4. remember the result of perseverance, the bliss of pliancy.

"By applying these four, your meditation will become pleasant and clear.

5. If you find yourself forgetting the instructions during meditation, apply continual mindfulness to keep them in mind.
6. Introspection is the antidote to laxity and excitement for it clearly distinguishes if they have arisen or not.
7. If they have arisen, the remedy is to immediately apply the antidotes.
8. If they are not present, don't apply any antidote but remain in an even, relaxed state.

"The nine mental placements to achieve calm abiding are as follows:

1. Placement: draw in the mind continually distracted by external objects and place it on the object of meditation.
2. Continual placement: continually place the mind on your chosen object to prevent it from being distracted to other objects.
3. Patch-like placement: recognize that through forgetfulness you are distracted and place your attention back onto its object, thereby 'patching up' your concentration.
4. Close placement: by continually drawing in the naturally vast mind, it becomes subtle.
5. Taming: by recalling the qualities of meditation, you develop a delight in it and thereby tame the mind.
6. Pacifying: having seen the faults of distraction, your dislike for meditation is pacified.
7. Thorough pacification: desire, mental unease, drowsiness, torpor, and so on, are thoroughly pacified.
8. Single-pointed placement: with great exertion, laxity and excite-

ment are discarded and your mind can now be placed single-pointedly on an object.

9. Even placement: being free of laxity and excitement, without even
the thought of exertion, you naturally enter into meditation that is
at once effortless and spontaneous, even and relaxed.

"The method of achieving calm abiding from the viewpoint of the six
powers is as follows:

1. If, depending on meditation instructions, you come to know the
methods for settling the mind and start to put them into practice,
you are engaging in the power of hearing.

2. When, through continually contemplating your mind in meditation, you can sustain a slight continuity of the practice, you have
achieved the power of contemplation.

3. The power of mindfulness is fully developed when you swiftly
identify distraction and bring the mind back to its object. Quickly
recognizing a loss of focus, through strong mindfulness, you refocus without distraction.

4. When your mindfulness is powerful and attention no longer distracted, you can use introspection like a spy to see whether faults
like laxity, excitement, and so forth, have arisen. Fully developed,
this is known as the power of introspection.

5. The power of enthusiasm is matured when although still prone
to subtle distraction, you are immediately aware of it, and with
further effort, you extend your meditation and free it from inter-
ruption, even in unfavorable conditions.

6. Finally the power of thorough familiarity arises when through
your exertions you become at one with the meditation. That
familiarity causes effortless samadhi to naturally occur.

"And the cultivation of calm abiding by means of the four mental engagements is as follows:

1. While practicing calm abiding, you are initially beset by laxity and
excitement and need a great effort to focus the mind and enter
samadhi. This is called focused mental engagement.

2. When your concentration is still interrupted by laxity and excite-

ment but you recognize and correct them as soon as they occur, you have reached interrupted mental engagement.

3. Eventually not even the slightest trace of laxity and excitement disturbs your concentration and you are able to sit in samadhi for long periods: you have progressed to uninterrupted mental engagement.

4. That becomes effortless mental engagement when you need minimal effort to enter an uninterrupted meditation and natural samadhi.

"The accomplishment of calm abiding in dependence upon mindfulness and introspection is as follows: Mindfulness means recalling the object of your meditation, such as the image of the Buddha, and holding it in your mind for as long as possible. Introspection immediately recognizes laxity and excitement during periods of weak mindfulness or at the onset of certain meditation experiences. It allows you to remove such faults and place your attention back onto the object of meditation with vivid mindfulness.

"Moreover if you are wondering exactly what these demons of laxity and excitement are: Subtle laxity occurs when the object becomes unclear even though the clarity of mind remains steady. With gross laxity, even the clarity is dull, and you fall into a heaviness of mind. In subtle excitement, a slight disturbance persists, although you are in no danger of losing the object of meditation. Gross excitement occurs when the mind scatters to objects of desire such as food, clothing, games, and so on. When laxity and excitement are strong, you'll need to muster your insight and only when they become weak may you relax a little.

"The signs of having achieved perfect calm abiding are as follows: your mind is free of both gross and subtle laxity and excitement, the visualized object of your meditation has become extremely clear and vivid, and you are able to meditate with a samadhi that is relaxed, even, and effortless, its stability now conjoined with the bliss of pliancy.

"A short and easy way for beginners to apply the instructions and develop calm abiding is to understand that the five hindrances can be condensed into the two, laxity and excitement, and the eight antidotes into mindfulness and introspection.

"Suffice it to say, the meaning of all the instructions from authentic scripture are included in the achievement of calm abiding by abandoning the five hindrances through applying the eight antidotes. If you were to learn all the various explanations, they would all help one another. So if you are serious in developing faultless calm abiding, it is essential that you know and cherish these precious treasures. When you put effort into cultivating calm abiding, know this: A samadhi at once free of both gross and subtle laxity and excitement and as immutable and stable as a mountain is a mere semblance of genuine calm abiding. Calm abiding is attained only when your samadhi is not only stable but also held by the bliss of mental and physical pliancy.

"After having achieved such a calm abiding, you will have the potential to deepen your insight and achieve a direct realization of emptiness. However, if you just practice calm abiding alone, you'll achieve all its qualities, which include clairvoyance and so on."

I sang:

> I supplicate my kind lamas,
> Pray bless me to achieve calm abiding, stable as a mountain!
>
> To dwell in a pleasant place, having few needs,
> Content, all activity abandoned,
> Ethical, and thoughts free of everything desirable,
> Are the causes to achieve calm abiding.
>
> When you first practice meditation, laziness will arise,
> At this time, recall samadhi's qualities, and develop confidence,
>    perseverance, and yearning.
> Remember that blissful pliancy comes from these,
> And you'll come to delight in the practice of samadhi.
>
> When you sit in meditation but forget the instructions, put strong
>    effort into recalling them,
> When laxity and excitement disturb your meditation, use
>    introspection to guard your mind;
> It is a fault not to apply the necessary antidotes, so apply them and
>    banish these demons!
>
> But when laxity and excitement are absent, let the antidotes also rest
>    and allow the mind to stay concentrated, in unruffled serenity and
>    peace.

Initially select an object,
An appropriate support for your practice,
Then place your mind perfectly upon it.
Don't let your attention wander,
But securely hold to your placement.
When distraction beguiles you,
Recalling that placement, patch it.
Place the mind close, and then tame it.
Pacifying, thoroughly pacifying, and passing through single-
    pointedness will lead you to tranquility.

Understand meditation through the power of hearing,
Practice through the power of contemplation,
The power of mindfulness helps if you forget,
And the power of introspection seeks out faults and removes
    them.
An unbroken flow of concentration dawns through the power of
    enthusiasm
And with the power of familiarity comes samadhi.

At meditation's outset, stay alert as a warrior—
You need focused mental engagement.
When your samadhi is beset with laxity and excitement and
    obstacles come by the dozen, employ interrupted mental
    engagement.
But when the power of these two and their cohorts is lost, practice
    uninterrupted mental engagement.
Then when the natural samadhi, an effortless mental engagement,
    dawns, you are close to winning calm abiding.

In essence, focus ceaselessly upon your support,
And vanquish laxity and excitement.
Then when your focus is clear and unwavering, know that serenity
    dawns with the obstacles gone,
And with an effort relaxed and unrelenting, sustain your meditation
    and you'll find an immovable and effortless samadhi.
Yet even though you now keep your focus for a long time, don't be
    fooled, this is just a facsimile.

For only when joined with a bliss of pliancy,
Not only of body but also of mind,
Can this be considered a true calm abiding,
Fully qualified and most amazing.

Depending on this, you can deepen insight and directly experience
    emptiness.
But even if this alone is your practice, you will soon develop qualities,
    like clairvoyance.

Through the lama's compassion, whatever merit I may have,
I dedicate to the actual realization of calm abiding.

# 15

# METHODS FOR ACHIEVING SPECIAL INSIGHT

My devoted, generous, and highly intelligent disciples Lobsang Tsering and the sublime emanation of past masters Lama Lobsang Chodrak of Tsegya Monastery,[1] both of whom had given up the concerns of this life, came to visit bringing many supplies. They prostrated with devotion and asked, "Precious Guru, the two of us would like to request a sublime instruction, one that combines both view and conduct, and would enable us to sever the continuity of samsara and ultimately become enlightened." They went on to summarize their request:

> Yogi, you are like the sun and moon.
> You fully reveal your compassionate face
> And illuminate the four continents of your students with the
>     unimpeded brilliance of your radiance—
> The fourfold skillful means with which you attract those to be
>     tamed.[2]

> Yogi in whom the three-kayas are spontaneously perfected,
> You are like a lion in whom the three powers are fully matured;[3]
> With your ruffled turquoise mane of experience and realization,
> You beautifully ornament the snowy peaks of the Buddha's
>     teachings.

> Yogi, you are a captain who sails his passenger-like disciples across
>     samsara's great ocean in a boat of compassion and skillful means.

> Yogi, you are like a physician, who, with the panaceas of profound
>     and vast instruction that you carry in your little medicine bag,
> Cures the emotional ills of all,
> Ushering in their well-being—enduring and strong.

Kye-hu! Alas! Since time without beginning we have been stricken
    with a life-threatening disease,
And continually experience a fluctuating temperature of attachment
    and aversion, which educes great pain.

With the labored breathing of praising myself and belittling others,
I feel nauseous at the sight of virtue's food.
Yet I quaff and become intoxicated on the wines of negativity,
And my illness rages still.

If a person with as many illnesses as I doesn't place himself in the
    care of a doctor, a spiritual friend, in whom else should he place
    his trust?

Eh ma! That such a lordly and regal doctor with pure karma and
    aspiration as you has arrived here is marvelous indeed.
Dispensing your medicine of the sublime Dharma,
You instantly clear the chronic disease of ignorance!

The minor and branch illnesses are gradually clearing,
And I have an appetite for virtue.
My mind is becoming virtuous and my complexion fair.

With the fortune to rise from the bed of samsara,
I have begun to walk the path to freedom with the fortune to never
    look back!

How kind you are, most regal of physicians!
You have given me the medicine of the Dharma and in return I shall
    endeavor to continually offer you the fruits of my practice.

However, should I once again fall under the sickness of the
    destructive emotions,
I will once again place my trust in you, master physician—
Kindly leave me a medicine that accords with the practice of the
    Kadampa masters of old,
A universal panacea, a single remedy, a single dose of which can cure
    confusion and destructive emotion and revive a patient's health.

Kindly grant the two of us a supreme medicine, a veritable deathless
    *amrita*:
The all-encompassing, pure, and undiluted instructions of the
    path—
the union of view and conduct.

I replied, "The two of you are most fortunate; listen without distraction to what I say and hold it well within your heart. Wandering in samsara, we do indeed experience myriad unwanted sufferings. Should you wonder whence they came, I shall illustrate their origin with a little story: A long time ago, there was a professor called Sherab Yudron, who was a very fearful fellow. One evening, he went out to teach, and on his way home, decided to offer a lamp at a local temple. A slight breeze caused the flame of his lamp to flicker and cast long shadows. The shadows fell upon a broom, and Sherab Yudron, mistaking the broom for a large scorpion, screamed! A local meditator, Geshe Yungwa Jungne, heard his cries and rushed to his aid. 'What's up?' he asked. 'Look there!' the teacher cried, and pointed toward the broom. He thought Geshe Yungwa Jungne very brave as he looked over toward the broom and strode over to investigate. 'You old fool,' the Geshe replied, 'it is simply a broom! There is nothing to be scared of!' Professor Sherab Yudron looked carefully, and seeing his mistake, they fell about laughing.

"All of samsara's many sufferings arise from a basic misunderstanding, confusion, or ignorance. Should you wonder what we are ignorant of, it is emptiness. We are ignorant and misunderstand the selves of both person and phenomena. If you reflect just how this has come to pass, imagine a man popping out in the dead of night, who in the darkness mistakes a coiled, mottled rope for a snake. Even though there is no snake, when mistakenly seeing the rope he reacts with such fear that he jumps back, clutching his chest. We are similarly impaired by the darkness of ignorance. The composite of our body and mind is like the mottled rope in the above example, and, when not seen clearly, the identity of an autonomous self is projected upon it to such an extent that it appears, like the snake in the above example, to exist solidly, as if it could be seen or handled. In dependence upon this basal confusion, the distinction of self and other appears, with an attachment for oneself and an aversion toward others—the dawning of desire and hatred. In dependence upon which, other destructive emotions come into being. This leads to action, an amassing of both good and bad karma, and the resultant development of the higher and lower realms of samsara.

"Our actions determine where within the higher and lower realms of samsara we shall wander and the level to which we will experience the many unwanted experiences of suffering—arising like the fear in the example of the rope being mistaken for a snake. The mighty Fifth Dalai Lama wrote:

> The thick darkness of ignorance causes the coiled mottled rope of
>    body and mind to appear as the poisonous snake of self,
> Resulting in the ensuing and ongoing fear—the threefold suffering.[4]

The Omniscient Panchen Lama, Lobsang Chokyi Gyaltsen said:

> The root of all suffering is ignorance. Ignorant of what you may wonder? Imagine a man, having mistaken a coiled rope for a poisonous snake, recoiling in great fear. Seeing his terror, a helpful friend rushes over and tells him not to be afraid for there is no snake, and he proceeds to explain why. The petrified man listens carefully to the reasons given by his friend, bends down to look carefully at the rope, and sees it for what it is, a rope. Having realized for himself that there is no snake before him, his fear subsides and he breathes a sigh of relief!

Similarly we apprehend that which is selfless as having an autonomous self and suffer greatly. A kind guru, a spiritual friend, using reason and spiritual quotation, then explains the selflessness of things to us in great detail; opening our wisdom eye, we investigate the nature of things for ourselves. Realizing both ourselves and every other phenomenon to be empty of an autonomous self, we can, as in the above example, breathe a sigh of relief as the fear and suffering of samsara naturally subsides and we achieve the bliss of liberation.

"Along with a perfect view of selflessness, a perfect conduct is required. A bird with only one strong wing isn't able to fly; a bird needs two wings to fly. Similarly, to achieve the liberation of omniscience, a union of two wings, view and conduct, is needed. If one is lacking, progress along the paths and grounds will not be made.

"Should you wonder how to practice a union of view and conduct, we should follow the sublime Kadampa masters of old who condensed the entire Buddhist canon into practical pith instructions. They understood the root of all suffering in samsara to be the ignorance that mistakes that which is without self as having a self. They resolved it using the reasoning of an absence of one and many, and realized the selflessness of both ourselves and phenomena.

"By practicing a meditative absorption that is like the sky and an illusory postmeditation is to practice a perfect union of view and conduct."

"All the time that we are alive, at this very moment, for example, and even in our dreams we continually have an idea of self. This notion is so strong and feels so solid; it is as if the self were tangible or visible. We don't believe the 'I' or 'self' to be a concept projected onto the composite of our body and mind but rather to exist there, in and of itself. If this were the case, the self would have to exist as one with or separate from the body/mind composite."

"Let us consider the body: it is made up of countless major and minor parts, whereas the mind is made up of myriad memories, anticipations, and the numerous and varied thoughts of the present moment. If the self were one with them all, given their multiplicity, there would be many selves!

"If not, and you insist that there is only one self that is 'one' with the body/mind aggregate, then its many parts and moments would be one, a singularity.

"If this is the case, distinctions such as 'I' and 'my,' 'my body' or 'my mind,' for example, cannot be used. When the body itself is created or decays, the self would be created and would decay. When the body is no more, the self would also cease. If you believe that, you'll waste your life and incur many faults. As such, it is clear that the 'I' is neither one with the body or the mind.

"Should you then wonder if the self is completely separate from the body and mind? Consider first the body. It is a composite of major parts, such as the four limbs, and myriad other, smaller, parts; bring each clearly to mind. Also, consider your thoughts: the present moment, past and future moments, and so on. The 'I' or self as a naturally existing entity isn't to be found anywhere; we simply find ourselves experiencing an utterly empty expanse.

"Reflect on any other phenomenon, your body, for example. Body is an idea projected onto a group of various parts: four limbs, torso, head, and so on; there is no inherently existent body. If there were, it would be either one with or separate from its parts.

"If the body were one with its parts it would follow that just as your body is composed of a head and four limbs, there would also be five bodies. Or else the five parts would have to be a single, partless thing. And if they were a singularity, there would no need to call them by different names: 'arm,' 'leg,' 'head,' and so on. Similarly, to stretch a limb would be to stretch the whole body; should this not be the case, it is a sign of their being separate. As you can see the body and its parts are not one and the same thing.

"As for the body and its parts being separate: separate out all the parts of your body, the four limbs, and so forth. Is there an independent body to be found? Use your wisdom of discrimination to look over everything. Besides the name 'body,' there isn't a molecule's worth of a tangible body to be found. Once again, you arrive at utter emptiness.

"What about the formless, you may wonder. Let's take the example of our mind. 'Mind' is a name given to an endless barrage of thoughts. If it existed as anything other, it would do so as either one with or other than those thoughts.

"If, as in the former case, mind and thoughts were one and the same, consider the inconceivable number of thoughts that flit through your head in a single day. Being one with thought, it would follow that you have an inconceivable number of minds. Similarly, if mind and thoughts were one and the same, memories of the past, anticipations of the future, and the thoughts of the present moment would all become a partless singularity. Also, if they were one, there would be no point in having two words: 'mind' and 'thought.'

"Memory and anticipation arise in dependence upon the present moment of thought; for these and many other reasons, to insist that mind and thoughts are one is to incur many faults. Thus we can see that the two are not one.

"Let us consider them to be completely separate. If we clearly look between thoughts of past, present, and future, besides a designated name, there isn't as much as a molecule's worth of an independent 'mind' to point to. One arrives at an empty yet awake state.

"Similarly, if you analyze and search for the inherent nature of anything within samsara and nirvana—Mount Meru, a house, whatever—besides a name, a mere convention, you'll discover only the utter emptiness of inherent existence.

"Having arrived at such certainty, rest in meditative equipoise within it. If dullness and agitation disturb your meditation and cause you to lose certainty, repeat the investigation. This time analyze the distractions, recognize their empty nature, and rest within the certainty of their utterly open, clear emptiness.

"Dullness, dimness, and drowsiness may assail you from time to time, as may a wildness of mind and copious thought. At these times, use the above method of analysis and a bright, clear recognition of their natural nonexistence or emptiness will dawn. When certain of it, rest within the experience in single-pointed meditative equipoise. These are the ways to protect and sustain the sky-like meditative equipoise.

"This is from the collected songs of the Seventh Dalai Lama, Kalsang Gyatso:

I pay homage to my kind guru,
He who is greater than even the gods and who is indivisible from
   Manjuvajra Tsongkhapa,
Who nakedly showed me the nature of mind—pure since the very
   beginning.

Dreams in the minds of those in the deepest of slumber,
And the horses and elephants conjured by a magician are mere
   appearances, conceptual constructs without any basis in reality.

Similarly, everything, be it self, other, samsara, or nirvana, exists
   insofar as there is a concept about it and it possesses a name.
Not the slightest thing can be found to exist truly in and of itself.

Yet, in confusion's deep slumber,
We ordinary folk perceive everything as true;
Just look how bad our mind is!

The 'I,' along with everything else that mistakenly appears to exist in
   and of itself,
Is that which is to be finally removed;
Its complete negation is crucial!

If the 'I' that is imputed to the aggregation of body and mind were
   not a mere 'name' and actually existed there,
It would do so independently and without reliance on the
   aggregation—
The two would be as unconnected as mountains in the east and west.

Moreover, in the face of such fine lines of reasoning such as the 'I'
    being one with the aggregates or other than them,
Being one with their cause or the effect thereof, and so forth,
It is found to be unobservable.

Having destroyed all reference points, an experience of a lucid, sky-
    like emptiness dawns—
This is wisdom, the absolute view.

Together with this, develop strong mindfulness, sharp introspection,
    and, using them to keep an eye on your meditation,
Develop a stable concentration, passing through the experiences of
    bliss, clarity, and nonthought.

Within the stability of single-pointed placement,
Analyze the self time and time again and a certainty with the
    strength of a vajra will be won,
A weapon as indestructible as Mount Meru with which to destroy
    the mountains of self-grasping—of this there is no doubt!

"That is how the meditation session should be practiced. When you enter into the postmeditation, you must realize that everything within both samsara and nirvana is essentially emptiness, pure from the very beginning, like the sky. Yet conventionally causes and conditions gather in a mutually dependent way and give rise to illusory, dreamlike appearances. The way in which these illusions appear without impediment is in exact accord with the unmistaken workings of karma, cause and effect. You must gain a strong confidence in the truth of this.

"To give up grasping at things as truly existing, abiding in and of themselves, meditate clearly on the empty appearance of things—their illusory, dreamlike nature. You realize, for example, how a magician conjures an illusion of elephants, horses, and so on. The spectacle is an illusion. The appearances are not considered to be truly existent, as such, neither feelings of attraction nor aversion arise. The same can be said for everything; self, other, and so forth, all are magical transformations.

"We need to recognize that nothing is established with true, self-existing characteristics; then notions of attraction and aversion will subside.

"Having achieved buddhahood, you will be able to emanate and transform as many form kayas as might be of benefit.

"Again, this is from the songs of Kalsang Gyatso:

> Within the equipoise of meditation, the mind should be pure as
>     space.
> Thereafter, during postmeditation, view the dependent arising of
>     things as rainbows.
> The appearances of the world are without substance, beautiful yet
>     illusory.
>
> Pleasure and pain are simply the play of dreams,
> Appearances are like images conjured up in an illusory town,
> And, sounds but echoes resounding in an empty cave—
> Tis' childish to grasp at them as real.
>
> When held before him, a mirror will clearly reflect a man's face;
> The empty, yet vivid reflection is undeniable.
> In a similar way, everything appears and is yet empty—
> It is simply their unmistaken and dependent nature.
>
> Observing the subtlest workings of karma—what to engage in and
>     what to avoid—
> And with strict observance of the three sets of vows,
> Should you neglect even to practice, happiness and liberation are still
>     close at hand!
>
> Recite these verses from time to time and make a concerted effort
>     at the conjoined view and conduct, the union of method and
>     wisdom.
>
> Before too long, the collections of merit and wisdom will be
>     perfected,
> The emotional and cognitive obscurations cleansed,
> And the dharma and rupakayas rendered evident,
> Ushering in a most wondrous benefit for both oneself and all
>     others."

The two of them were very happy with what I taught and rejoiced greatly.
After making prostrations, they returned home.

# THE NEED FOR BOTH CALM ABIDING AND SPECIAL INSIGHT

The teacher of Bon-ri Tulku,[1] the emanated virtuous friend Phuntsok, a fine lama—a veritable lord possessing myriad qualities of scriptural learning and realization—asked me for a practical instruction to actualize calm abiding and special insight. He insisted that it be both short and concise and from an authentic source. He then sang a most excellent exhortation:

> Giving those bereft of the Dharma what they desire,
> The vast and profound teachings,
> Lordly master, you are like a wish-fulfilling jewel!
> Respectfully, I offer you obeisance.
>
> Freed from the selfish fetters of self-grasping,
> And well trained in the altruistic mind of enlightenment,
> Having transformed the dualism by means of the Dharma,
> Lordly guru, you have fulfilled your aspirations!
>
> As for myself, since time without beginning, I have lived in the house
>     of the three worlds:
> I spread myself out on the mattress of self-grasping,
> And cover myself with the blankets of the experiences of pleasure,
>     pain, and equality.
>
> I lay my head upon the pillow of the eight worldly concerns,
> And fall into the deep sleep of ignorance.
> When the wretched habitual tendencies stir, I dream.
> Continually in a state of troubled sleep and nightmare,
> Is there no chance to awaken?

Most wondrous and compassionate lord, won't you beat your great
  and divine drum of the profound and vast teachings?
Awaken me from confusion's slumber, and put an end to these
  nightmares.

Gracious and lordly master,
Until fully awake, I shall continually besiege you!

Compassionate guru, through your great love,
Pray grant me a short, concise, and authentic instruction in the
  practical application of both calm abiding and special insight.

I replied, "The second Buddha, the great and unequaled Atisha, was born
into the royal family of Bengal[2]—the wealth of which was said to have
even rivaled the ancient kings of Eastern China. In India, it was reported,
and in Tibet, it was clearly evident that he was well versed in the five sciences,[3] adept in ethics, concentration, and wisdom—the essence of the three
baskets,[4] and displayed the signs of spiritual realization of the generation
and perfection phases of the four classes of tantra,[5] such as while circum-
ambulating and prostrating to the temples, his feet didn't even touch the
ground; he displayed clairvoyance; performed miracles; and so on. In fact
he possessed all the myriad qualities found within spiritual realization. He
perceived the faces of the Venerable Tara and other meditational deities,
as numerous as stars in the night sky, and he received their teachings and
prophecies.

"However, Atisha's banner of renown was only hoisted and waved
throughout the three worlds after his arriving in Tibet, where, in response
to a request made by Lha Lama Jangchub O and others for a book—a veritable treasure trove of teachings—he composed the incomparable work *A
Lamp for the Path to Enlightenment*. With this, along with his other accomplishments, it is clear that his deeds were greater here in Tibet than in India.
He was a veritable sun of the Buddha's teachings, who cleared away Tibet's
darkness.

"This book is the mother of all lam-rim treatises, including *The Greater
and Smaller Stages of the Path*. Should I even search, I doubt whether I could
find a greater or more authentic source of the Dharma! Within its pages,
we find the way to train in calm abiding—the essence of concentration—as
follows:

All buddhas say the cause of perfecting the twofold accumulation of
merit and wisdom rests solely on the development of clairvoyance.

Those without the power of clairvoyance cannot work for the benefit
of all,
Just as a bird with undeveloped wings cannot soar in the sky.

The merit gained in a single day by one with such clairvoyance—
Even in a hundred lifetimes—cannot be obtained by one with
without.

Those who'd like to quickly complete the collections and achieve
buddhahood must first achieve clairvoyance:
Which is won through effort and not by sloth.

Without the accomplishment of calm abiding, clairvoyance will not
arise;
Therefore make repeated efforts to achieve it.

Without the requisites for calm abiding, stabilization will not be won,
Even if you were to make great efforts at meditation for a thousand
years!

Therefore know well the requisites from *The Requisites for Meditative
Stabilization Chapter*,⁶ and place your mind upon a virtuous
object.

Once a yogi has achieved calm abiding, clairvoyance will also be
theirs.

"Therefore, whether it's accumulating merit and wisdom, or accomplishing the welfare of self and others, great progress can be made if we have
clairvoyance. Clairvoyance arises from calm abiding, which is won through
diligence, not laziness. Therefore it is essential to apply a continual effort
until calm abiding is attained because without it clairvoyance will not be
achieved.

"As we are taught, without its requisites, calm abiding will not be attained
even if we meditate for a very long time. Therefore, as mentioned in *The Req-*

*uisites for Meditative Stabilization Chapter*, the requisites are elimination, preparation, desisting, stopping the misery, aversion, recalling the qualities, effort, unifying, and the means for stability.[7]

"Moreover, the *Hearer Levels* lists thirteen requisites for calm abiding;[8] you would do well to know these and apply them. Among all of these requisites, the most crucial are morality, having few wants, contentment, and seclusion.

"Having gathered them together, sit comfortably in either the seven-point posture or at least cross-legged and straighten your back. Without any distraction, focus your mind on a virtuous object, such as an image of the Buddha, and hold it there. In the early stages of practice, you may need to continually refocus on the image, but gradually and with perseverance, you'll be able to hold the image in your mind without forgetting it. Thereafter, be careful not to lose your mindfulness of the object to laxity or excitement; be vigilant, as soon as they arise, redouble your efforts to focus on the image. Through these efforts, your practice of introspection and mindfulness will become sustained, and one day you'll be free of both laxity and excitement. At that time, you will have achieved the fully qualified calm abiding along with a blissful mental and physical pliancy. You'll also achieve clairvoyance at that time.

"Furthermore, in Atisha's beautiful text, we also find methods for training in special insight—the essence of wisdom—as follows:

> Through realizing the aggregates, constituents, and sources are not
> produced,
> Their natural emptiness is known—this is said to be wisdom.

> Something existent cannot be produced,
> Nor something nonexistent, like a sky flower,
> Because both of these errors are ridiculous.
> Production from them both is likewise impossible.

> Nothing is produced from itself,
> Nor from another, or both;
> And because it wasn't produced causelessly,
> It does not exist inherently—by means of its entity.

Moreover if you investigate things using the reasoning of singularity
    or plurality,
You'll see that their entity is unobservable and will gain certainty in
    their natural nonexistence.

*The Seventy Stanzas on Emptiness*, *The Root Stanzas on the Middle
    Way*, and other texts,
All explain the nature of things to be established as emptiness.

There are a great number of treatises, but I have not elaborated upon
    them here.
I have merely explained their conclusions for the purpose of
    meditation.

Since the nature of all phenomena without exception is
    unobservable, they are selfless.
To meditate thereupon is to meditate upon wisdom.

As wisdom doesn't see an inherent nature in anything,
Analyze wisdom itself and meditate thereupon—free of all concepts.

The world has arisen from our thoughts and its nature is conceptual.
To be free of such concepts, is nirvana supreme.

As the Buddha said:

> The great confusion of thought causes your fall into
>     samsara's ocean.
> Abiding in the concentration beyond thought—
> The space-like nonconceptuality becomes ever clear.

From the *Mnemonic, Entering the Nonconceptual*:

> When bodhisattvas nonconceptually contemplate this
>     profound Dharma,
> They eventually go beyond all concepts—so difficult to
>     transcend—
> And achieve the nonconceptual.

And:

> Having ascertained through reasoning and citation
>   that phenomena are neither produced nor inherently
>   existent, meditate, free of all concepts.
>
> If you are able to do so, you'll pass serially through the
>   level of warmth[9] and the rest;
> Eventually you'll come to the grounds, such as Rapture[10]
>   and the others.
> Know then that buddhahood does not lie far away.

"Initially gather the causes for special insight: continually listen to a qualified guru's instructions and contemplate them deeply. Supplicate the guru as inseparable from your sublime deity and make continuous effort to accumulate merit and purify the negative karma you have previously accumulated. Go to an isolated place, sit comfortably with your back straight, and contemplate how your aggregates, constituents, sources, and so on, in fact all phenomena, are not produced. Come to know how they are naturally empty. This then is wisdom and the way to produce it is as follows:

"Your aggregates, constituents, sources, in fact all phenomena in samsara and nirvana, are not produced; they are naturally emptiness. This recognition is called wisdom.

"The way to recognize emptiness is as follows: Consider all sights and sounds—everything that appears and exists within samsara and nirvana, your aggregates, constituents, sources, and so on. If they actually arose from something...

1. Let's take a sprout as our example: if the sprout existed at the time of its cause, a seed, it would have already come into existence and would not need to grow again. If you say it does need to grow again, why? Growth has lost its meaning and there would be an infinite regress of 'needing to grow.'
2. If you believe that the sprout grew from nothing, it would lead to the absurd consequence that something could arise from nothing; with flowers growing in the sky, and so forth.
3. The idea that it arose from both something and nothing is negated as a natural consequence of the former two reasons.
4. And lastly, do you think that the sprout arose from neither something nor nothing? Well, if when nothing is seen to have previously grown, future growth is impossible.

"If you analyze along these lines, you'll recognize how nothing 'grows' and how all is naturally emptiness.

1. Should you wonder if something, be it animate or inanimate, grew from itself—it didn't. Let's take the example of a man; he wasn't born from himself, was he? If he was, then who is the father and who the son, as they are one and the same!

2. Perhaps he was born from another. If a baby were born from the fertilized egg of his mother, at the time of the cause, the fertilized egg, the result, the child, would have to be seen; but he isn't. What if he was born from another, one with whom he has no actual connection? If that were the case, hands could grow from legs and feet from arms; water could arise from fire and fire from water, and so on. Chaos—where anything goes, and effects don't need to rely upon their concordant causes!

3. Was he born from both himself and another? Well, we analyzed his birth from both himself and another earlier, right? The refutations of each can be applied here.

4. Perhaps you should consider his being born causelessly. If that were the case, farmers wouldn't need to plough and sow their fields, as the crops would simply spring up in them! Needless to say, this isn't the case.

"Using these lines of reasoning, you'll come to realize how everything, whether an inner or an outer phenomenon, is naturally empty of inherent existence.

"Moreover, phenomena aren't single unrelated things; they are the sum of their parts. Neither are they a multiplicity, for when each part is removed, the thing itself disappears, it cannot be found.

"The reasoning used in *The Seventy Stanzas on Emptiness*, *The Root Stanzas on the Middle Way*, and in many other works explains how everything has always been emptiness. You should read as many of them as possible and resolve your understanding. Don't simply use them as a reference; utilize these quotations and lines of reasoning and come to a definitive conclusion concerning emptiness, as these writings explain the meaning of meditation on selflessness very well.

"Having understood this, as before, when you used lines of reasoning to analyze and concluded that there isn't so much as an atom's worth of autonomous existence to be seen, that everything is emptiness, repeat this analysis again and again, and meditate. This is wisdom, what it actually means to meditate on emptiness.

"Moreover, having analyzed and gained certainty that everything is naturally empty, perhaps you will wonder, 'Shouldn't I give up grasping after this wisdom of the meditation on emptiness?'

"Reflect that naturally, when objects of genuine wisdom are searched for, they are not found. Similarly, if wisdom itself is analyzed using the same reasoning, it will also be recognized as nonexistent.

"Eventually, you'll overcome concepts and gain certainty, and this will cause a nonconceptual wisdom to dawn. Within this experience, everything, be it objective or subjective, is realized to be nothing other than emptiness and any idea of something being other than emptiness is immediately cut off.

"The necessity for nonconceptual meditation is taught widely in the statements of many sutras and tantras. Make use of these statements and the different lines of reasoning and gain confidence that all dharmas are unborn and naturally nonexistent. Within this experience, you'll understand how all thoughts are not other than emptiness.

"I have given brief and concise instructions enabling you to meditate on emptiness and spoken of its necessity. If you meditate accordingly, you will gradually make progress, passing through the level of warmth[11] and so on, to the first ground, Supreme Joy.[12] You'll pass through these levels serially and before too long will awaken as Buddha."

# 17

# How to Practice a Union of Relative and Ultimate Bodhichitta

My fortunate disciple Lobsang Tenzin requested, "Precious guru, the principal meditation you employ quickly softens even the most stubborn of minds. Please teach me such an uncommon and extremely profound instruction." He went on:

> Having arrived before you and with single-pointed respect, I prostrate.
> Father, kinder than all buddhas,
> Pray lend me your ear and listen to my request.

> In youth, I was distracted by play,
> In life's middle, I was seduced by wealth,
> And now, who knows how much time remains?

> From birth I have witnessed many die—the elderly as well as the young.
> As for myself, I know I'll die, but I know not when.
> This very night? The danger is always there.

> Reflecting so, O protector, I sought you out.
> Having been accepted as the lowliest of the father guru's disciples,
> I reflected on the profound Dharma of emptiness,
> The sharp weapon to cut down the vile enemy of self-grasping,
> And wondered how to wield it and subdue the unruly mind?

> Lacking the realization of the essence of mind to be dharmakaya,
> I remain confused and wander aimlessly in samsara,
> Continually oppressed by the strong sicknesses of the afflictive
>     emotions.
> Master physician, I beg you for a strong remedy!

Root guru, my protector, you are Vajradhara in person and hold all
the profound pith instructions in the palm of your hand.
With your great loving concern, pray grant me a most profound
teaching.

I will practice in exact accord with your instructions.
Pray grant me the protection of your prayers—freedom from
obstacles and error—
And bless me that before too long I will give rise to extraordinary
experience and realization.

I replied, "In the root verses of mind training that he presented to Atisha,
the master of bodhichitta Serlingpa said:

Appearances in dreams indicate the nature of mind.
Mind itself is an illusion; realize it to be just so, empty.
Like clouds of various shapes, everything arises within emptiness,
And the two are inseparable like water bubbles and water.
As such, all is like the sky, indescribable, and beyond elaboration.

"To meditate upon ultimate bodhichitta, retire to an isolated spot. Sit up
straight on a comfortable seat, take refuge, develop bodhichitta, and supplicate your guru. The example of the dream establishes appearances to be
mind. The example of an illusion establishes mind itself as being empty. The
example of clouds establishes appearances arising from within emptiness.
The example of water bubbles establishes the inseparability of appearances
and emptiness. The example of the sky establishes the inexpressible, beyond
all elaboration.

"Having understood these metaphors, meditate in an equipoise that is
free from all elaboration, like the sky. At the conclusion, make prayers of
dedication.

"During postmeditation, see everything as empty appearances, dreamlike and illusory. Meditate on love and compassion for those who fail to
realize this, and make efforts at cherishing others more highly than yourself.
Practicing like this, you'll swiftly awaken to buddhahood. To summarize:

Sit up straight upon a comfortable cushion, take refuge, develop
bodhichitta, and supplicate your guru.

Like dreams, everything is found to be your mind.
Like illusions, mind itself is found to be emptiness.
Like clouds in the sky, everything is found to arise from within
  emptiness.
Like water bubbles, appearances and emptiness are found to be
  indivisible.
And like the example of the sky—
Ultimately everything is found to be beyond expression and
  elaboration.

Having understood these metaphors, settle into a meditation free of
  all elaboration.
Afterward make prayers of dedication.

During postmeditation realize all phenomena are illusory.
Meditate upon love and compassion for those who do not recognize
  this and wander aimlessly in samsara.

Take their loss and defeat continually upon yourself and offer them
  your profit and victories.
You should not only practice giving and taking as contemplation, but
  enact it to the best of your ability.

"This is the way to practice a union of the two bodhichittas, relative and
ultimate; it will not leave you in samsara nor in nirvana but will deliver you
to the state of omniscience, buddhahood."

# 18

## ULTIMATE BODHICHITTA

My disciple Ngawong Yeshe, a fully ordained monk of Thoding Monastery, is a most fortunate student, one who has all the qualities of an authentic disciple as stipulated in the sutras and tantras. He often comes to visit me accompanied by the chanting master of Tashi Gang, Zurpa Lobsang Tsultrim, Lobsang Gelek, and Lobsang Tenzin. The four of them have shown me great kindness and offered representations of enlightened body, speech, and mind, as well as much gold, silver, tea, butter, clothing, silks, and many other things as well.

The four of them came to visit one day and brought rice and dried fruits in cups of the finest china. The monk Ngawong Yeshe went on to address me in an extremely respectful way, "Precious root guru, our refuge and protector, you who are kinder to us than any buddha, you are our spiritual friend—one who is impartial and equally friendly to all; pray grant us a moment of your time. The four of us have been contemplating birth, death, the sufferings of samsara, and are feeling slightly ill at ease. However, the mere sight of your face, great and revered captain—you who liberate from samsara's vast oceans—has cheered us greatly.

"When listening to your nectar-like speech, there is no doubt left as to our potential for achieving liberation and omniscience—provided we practice your instructions, of course! This has given rise to an all-pervading sense of joy and bliss not experienced before.

"We have heard that you have given many of your fortunate disciples, both monastic and lay, pith instructions, songs of advice and experience. You, kind guru, are like the sun, who, with your warm rays of compassion, may well set in one place but will move on to work for the benefit of beings in another. In other words, having enjoyed the golden sunlight of your compassion, the four of us realize that we will not be ever bathed in its warmth. Nevertheless, we four vajra-siblings are now gathered before you and request that you, in your great compassion, grant us a profound pith instruction." He sang:

The accumulations of merit and wisdom are perfected within
    concentration:
Meditative equipoise, vast, like the sky,
And postmeditation, where everything appears as illusory.

To realize everything to be the play of mind and that mind itself to
    be empty
Is to recognize that all phenomena appear distinctly and without
    confusion within emptiness/clarity.

Without moving from the basic space of the dharmakaya,
The rupakaya appears to benefit beings and, until samsara is emptied,
    will work tirelessly for them.
Refuge and protector, our wish-fulfilling jewel,
Lend us your ear a while.
We four vajra-siblings have been thinking . . .

This human form we have is like a deer, which, from the moment of
    its birth, has been continually pursued by a hunter, time.
Driven forward by the dogs that desire her flesh and fats,
She has become old, with shortness of breath, and quivering calf.
The arrow of illness having pierced her lung,
She approaches the edge of death's precipice.

Reflecting thus has brought us great fear.

To fall into the fire pits of the three lower realms is to experience a
    suffering almost impossible to endure,
Whereas birth in the higher realms of gods and men is temporary
    and inevitably leads to a fall.
Alas, there is no enduring bliss to be had!

To acquire possessions through illicit means is as if to have quaffed
    poison and cut the very life force of liberation.
To reflect again and again on these sufferings is to induce a great fear,
    each one greater than the last.

Considering what might be done, I met you, my lordly ferryman,
Who, in your great boat of compassion, leads us across the poisonous
    waters of samsara to the pleasant city of liberation.
Reflecting on the fortune of those guided by you brings great joy to
    my mind.


Protector, the nectar of your instruction quenches the thirst of those
    desirous of the Dharma and instantly fulfills their wishes.
Oh, what a joy, an absolute delight!


Precious guru, having made requests and thinking only of you,
May we follow and be ever held by you.
Until we all awaken, may we never be apart!


Pray grant us four vajra brothers a profound oral instruction, the
    mere sound of which prevents a fall to the lower realms,
And meditation upon which prevents wandering in samsara.


I replied, "Listen well, fortunate ones. The term 'oral instruction' refers to an instruction originating with the perfect Buddha that has been handed down orally through a lineage of sublime persons. These instructions were refined as they were practiced over the years, resulting in such pith instructions as the graduated stages of the path (*lam-rim*) and mind training (*lo-jong*), taken as they are from the vast and profound discourses of Buddha. I have received these instructions, and if I relate them to you, it is acceptable to say that they have become my 'oral instructions.'

"I have nothing other than these instructions to offer; no new or unique Dharma. After having received such instructions, you must practice them according to their respective traditions.

"If something is important, like *The Hundred Thousand Verse Perfection of Wisdom Sutra*, for example, it may be read aloud a hundred times and yet the meaning still remains vague. I'll now remind you of the important points of what I have previously taught; please listen carefully.

"Understand that in these decadent times life is short and the time of death uncertain. There are also many things you might like to know, which leave little time for practice. As such, the sole sufficient Dharma to swiftly deliver you to the omniscient state of complete and perfect buddhahood is the precious ultimate bodhichitta—the experience that is essentially emptiness and clarity conjoined. Free of all grasping, it is a great and utter openness—the ground of both samsara and nirvana.

"With a strong sustained mindfulness, which is all-pervasive, relaxed, and serene, one that doesn't hold on to or reject anything, remain within this great, vast expanse that is free from all extremes, the dharmakaya. You will in turn awaken from the darkness of afflictive emotions, grasping, and concepts. One day before too long, enlightenment will be yours.

"Once the natural state, the vast sky-like expanse of emptiness/clarity conjoined, is rendered evident, the subtle obscurations of center and periphery will be cleared.

"It is essential to mix appearances with mind. Appearances are neither outside of you, nor are they inside mind itself; emptiness isn't obscured by appearances, and they in turn aren't blocked by emptiness.

"Once a conviction of the great expanse, the union of appearance and emptiness, has dawned, remain within it.

"To do this will cut the eighty-four thousand destructive emotions at their root, the meaning of the eighty-four thousand dharma teachings will appear clearly in your mind, and everything within samsara and nirvana will appear as if a drama. To know this Dharma is to free all.

"As such, the guru who reveals it to you is kinder that any buddha; indeed, they should be viewed as the very embodiment of all buddhas. With the greatest of devotion, you should supplicate such a master from the very depths of your heart. As it is said:

> Within the emptiness of bliss, clarity and nonthought, the guru's
> mind is like the sky.

And:

> Profound wisdom is as vast as space.

Supplicate the guru in various ways—always clearly and from the very depths of your heart. As the quotes say, the guru's mind, the dharmakaya, is as vast as the sky. It abides clearly, continually, pervading both samsara and nirvana. It is unbiased clarity and emptiness, free of all elaboration and notions of time and change. Mingle your mind with this wisdom—like space merging with space.

"Once they are mixed and you have given rise to a great concentration, a meditative absorption that is as vast as the sky, sustain it such that you continue to experience it continually day and night.

"Should you get distracted, loosen the meditation, begin to despair, supplicate your guru, mix your mind with his, and once again begin the single-pointed practice of meditation in a carefree and relaxed way.

"Similarly, if torpor, dullness, and drowsiness strike, raise your voice and supplicate the guru in melodious tones.

"Awareness is like the sky—dismiss any notion of direction—expand, elevate, and heighten it. Experience an expansive openness, and fill it with a relaxed, all-embracing mindfulness, and, no matter what may happen, you must sustain this awareness without the slightest distraction. This is what is referred to as the regal guard."

I summarized in verse:

Within that emptiness of bliss, clarity, and nonthought,
I supplicate the vast, sky-like mind of the guru that perfectly abides
    as the three liberations.[1]

I supplicate the mind of all buddhas:
Realization equal to the extent of space,
All-pervasive and permeating both samsara and nirvana,
Vivid, and unobscured by any notion of time.

Limitless buddha fields abide in the purity of mind itself, the
    dharmadhatu.
Bless me such that my mind may merge with this exalted mind of the
    guru and all buddhas.

My guru's discernment churned the ocean of milk that is the sutras,
    tantras, and shastras to produce the butter of quintessential
    instructions,
Which he kindly shared with me.
The door to the jewel treasury of mind itself—
Source of both common and uncommon accomplishments—
Was unlocked with the key of the guru's instructions and fulfilled
    the aims of one and all.

The dramas of samsara and nirvana are played out in the pure realm
that is the dharmadhatu of mind.
It is truly the greatest of spectacles, the likes of which have never
before been seen in this world.

The source of everything in samsara and nirvana is the sky-like
nature of mind,
A spacious expanse with neither direction nor partiality.
It cannot be won by exertion, but rather by relaxation.

Whatever arises, be it good or bad, doesn't exist outside of yourself.
The natural forms of the emptiness of mind itself appear like
reflections in a mirror

Mind itself is the ground of all—
If anything appears within it, it doesn't exist.
It is like the outer sky, vast and spacious, pervading and permeating
both samsara and nirvana.
Suchness completely pervades all.
It is impossible to conceive of it as this or that,
Or to point to its center or border.
Let go and relax within this expanse and experience that which is
unchanging and vivid, like the sky.

Do not attempt to carefully divide the great all-pervading
dharmadhatu into sections.
It would be like trying to measure space;
The attempt will only cause you obscuration.

Essentially, everything that arises is the display of mind,
And mind itself is empty luminosity; rest therein.
If unpleasant things occur, don't get stressed,
Simply remain open and completely at ease.

If you can sustain meditative equipoise within the spacious,
unfragmented, undivided, and all-pervading nature of emptiness
and clarity,
You'll completely purify adventitious emotion and conception,
The meaning of Dharma words will arise from within,

You'll see samsara and nirvana as if a show,
And you'll fulfill the twofold benefit of self and other.

In dependence upon supreme, ultimate bodhichitta, the dharmakaya
  is rendered evident,
And without moving therefrom, may the rupakaya fulfill the wishes
  of all beings.

## GIVING AND TAKING

My student Lobsang Gelek then said, "Merely through hearing your profound oral instructions on ultimate bodhichitta, my awareness has become lucid and spacious; I feel this to be an experience of insight for which I'm extremely grateful. Kindly now grant an instruction for the practice of the precious relative bodhichitta, to be used once meditative equipoise is concluded." I offered him the following reply:

Eh ma! Fortunate child of the lineage:
Indivisible awareness, clarity and emptiness, is ultimate bodhichitta,
  free from all elaboration;
Meditate on this boundless, empty lucidity.

Thereafter understand that confusion concerning this natural state is
  ignorance.
Ignorance gives rise to afflictive emotions,
Which give rise to negative action,
Causing unpleasant birth,
Leading to the immeasurable sufferings of samsara.

Pitiful sentient beings, all of whom without any exceptions have
  been parents to you
And have shown you exceptional kindness, continually suffer these
  miseries.

Develop empathy and compassion for them.
Resolve to end their suffering and place them in bliss,
And to this end, practice giving and taking utilizing the breath:
When you inhale, take all beings' suffering, negative karma, and
  emotion into yourself in the form of black smoke.

Once it has entered inside, imagine that it dissolves into your heart
and puts an end to any notion of self-grasping.
Consider the suffering, negative karma, and emotions of all parent
beings to be completely gone.

When you exhale, give the entirety of your happiness and virtue to
all beings in the form of white smoke.
It enters their bodies, and they become pervaded with physical and
mental bliss.

Imagine that they become blessed and imbued with temporal happiness,
And that ultimately they will awaken to buddhahood.

The *Precious Garland* says:

May their negative ripen upon me,
And may my virtue ripen upon them.

Panchen Sakya Shri says:

If happy, dedicate your joy to all, and may benefit and bliss pervade
the sky!
If sad, take the misery of all upon yourself, and with this, may the
ocean of suffering dry up!

Make these and other such prayers of dedication and, should you desire to
awaken to buddhahood quickly, practice well these instructions of relative
bodhichitta.

## DO THE SUFFERINGS OF OTHERS TAKEN UPON ONESELF NEED TO BE PURIFIED?

My student Lobsang Tenzin asked, "The sufferings of others that you have
taken upon yourself shouldn't be purified, should they?"
"They shouldn't." I replied:

The auspicious and mutually dependent activities of the bodhisattvas
transform suffering into bliss,
Just as an alchemical formula transforms iron into gold.

The twofold bodhichitta has the ability to transform the suffering
  taken from others and turn it into bliss,
Just as the stomach of a peacock has the ability to digest poison and
  transform it into a nutrient.

Despite its filth, crops grow well in a field well fertilized with manure.
Similarly, if you're able to endure the sufferings taken upon yourself,
  buddhahood is close at hand.

When dried grass and kindling is thrown onto a blazing fire, the
  flames instantly consume them.
Illness and negative circumstance are similarly embraced by a
  practitioner of ultimate and relative bodhichitta.

When a full peacock comes across poison, she will devour it.
A bodhisattva filled with the sufferings of others will not abandon
  them but will similarly gorge himself.

If suffering doesn't arise as bliss, get rid of it.
What is there to say about taking it from others?
However, when suffering is experienced as bliss,
The words "give it up" have no meaning!

Just as there is no real suffering to be either taken up or abandoned
  in a dream,
The essence of suffering is primordially empty.
And within emptiness, what is there to take up or abandon?

There is no suffering to give up,
Yet thinking there is leads to the idea of abandoning its cause.
Happiness and suffering are essentially and primordially empty,
Yet they do appear; like illusions.

Illusory horses, elephants, and so on, are conjured by a magician.
Similarly, the phenomena of happiness and suffering, good and bad,
  environments and beings are all conjured by the mind.

The conjuring mind itself is primordially empty—
An empty clarity as vast as the sky itself.

To rest within this is to experience ultimate bodhichitta,
And happiness and well-being will rise like the sun.

If you realize this, there will be no need to abandon any sufferings
    you have taken upon yourself.
Should you even want to, there is nothing to find.

Within the expanse of ultimate bodhichitta, the word "suffering"
    doesn't exist.
Within suchness itself, there is a natural joy and happiness.
This is the resting place of the yogin.

Lobsang Tsultrim then said, "What you say is very true. Having actualized the ultimate, natural state, suffering is indeed experienced as happiness. Illnesses, demons, and so on, need not be shunned as a yogin can wear then as ornaments. Milarepa said:

Illnesses, demons, misdeeds, and defilements ornament and beautify
    a yogin.[2]

And:

There may be a means to eliminate the great ornament of sickness,
    but what's the point?

He also said:

May I take and purify all of your sufferings.

Could you teach those of us who haven't realized the natural state of reality a means of purifying the illusory, dreamlike sufferings of others that we take upon ourselves, so that when illness and such befall us it is of even greater benefit?"

I replied that it is perfectly alright to purify suffering and offered this as a means to do so:

Eh ma! Fortunate child of the lineage!
To completely purify the suffering of others that you take upon
    yourself when you are ill and other such times, do this:

As you exhale, imagine all the suffering that you have taken upon
yourself in the form of black light.
It gently dissolves into space, earth, or rocks, whatever is before you,
and disappears into emptiness.
Have the conviction that all illnesses, negative actions, and
obscurations are purified.

Inhale all the blessings of the buddhas of the ten direction in the
form of white light.
It dissolves into your body, and you glow with a healthy radiance.

Now visualize yourself as a yidam deity.
Imagine an inconceivable light and numerous offering goddesses
emanate from the seed-syllable and mantra garland at your
heart.
Carried on the exhalation of your breath,
They emerge to proffer offerings to the five senses of all buddhas and
bodhisattvas throughout the ten directions.

As you inhale, imagine the blessings of the body, speech, and mind of
the inconceivable buddhas of the ten directions,
In the aspect of your yidam's form, mantra garland, and hand
implements,
Dissolve into you like snowflakes into a lake, and you will attain the
rainbow body—a kaya of light.

This time, as you exhale, imagine inconceivable light emanates from
you.
It strikes the environment and all who dwell in it, purifying them of
all impurity, imperfection, and fault.
The world now appears as a pure land and all beings as divinities.

When you inhale, imagine the vitality of both the environment and
beings in the aspect of the nectar of immortality.
It dissolves into you, and you become an awareness holder with
power over life.

Involve others by practicing like this:

When you inhale, imagine the blessings of the gurus and buddhas
    come to abide within you;
As you exhale, sentient beings receive the virtue and happiness you
    offer.

If you continually practice taking the suffering of others upon
    yourself, along with the methods purification,
You'll eventually be able to actually take the pain of others upon
    yourself.
Should it not be possible to change someone's immediate experience,
    you must then change the environment.

Just as the beauty of a peacock's plumage intensifies the more she
    gorges on virulent poison,
Your practice of giving, taking, and purification will result in the
    kaya beautified with the marks and signs of buddhahood.

They were delighted with my reply and told me that these methods would
help them greatly. After offering prostrations, they returned home.

# 19

## MAHAMUDRA

*A Teaching on the Nature of Mind, Based on the Songs of Milarepa*

---

My disciple, the extremely devout, vastly intelligent doctor and scholar of medicines Lhaje Chogyal, gave me much food—fruits, rice, and so forth. He offered me a stainless silk scarf and requested instruction with the following:

> Generally speaking, you are a spiritual friend to all,
> But to me you are a constant source of refuge.
> Root guru, Vajradhara, most regal—
> Look upon your child with eyes of compassion.
>
> Protector of the dharma treasury, you have spoken much of the
>     profound and vast dharmas:
> Of a provisional meaning, relating to cause and effect,
> And of the ultimate, introductions pointing to the nature of mind
>     and so on.
>
> Having fallen under the influence of attachment and aversion,
> I've engaged in the ten nonvirtuous deeds.
> In your divine presence, guru most precious,
> I worry as I have neither shame nor fear of falling to the three lower
>     realms—
> Pray look upon this rotten-hearted vagabond with compassion!
>
> In the earlier part of my life, I was obsessed with food and clothing,
> I ate all day, slept all night, and delighted in the breaking of vows and
>     samaya.
>
> Now that I come to practice the divine Dharma,
> I realize that the summer sun warms all as she sits proudly in the sky,
>     and the winter winds freeze all they caress,

I think myself a practitioner, but to miss a single meal leads me to
think I'm at death's door!
Pray look upon this humble vagabond with compassion.

Pray grant me some beneficial instructions, to protect and change my
attitude—
Something to immediately soften my rigid mind!
To this effect, grant your blessing.

I replied, "In dependence on the profound and crucial points of your guru's
instruction, along with reasoning and quotation from scripture, investigate
the root of all phenomena, that which pervades both samsara and nirvana
without partiality—the nature of mind. You need to see it nakedly, just as
it is: an empty lucidity, utterly open and beyond grasping, an all-pervasive
expanse that is like the sky—beyond all elaboration. As Milarepa said:

I, Milarepa, a yogi, look directly into things and see their essence,
which is like the sky, beyond any elaboration.
When attempting to settle within this state even a beginner must be
skilled in meditation.

He went on:

When I meditate on Mahamudra, the great seal,
I simply relax effortlessly upon the natural state.

"That's it. There isn't any indication of amorphous meditation, or of sink-
ing into a vague, oblivious state. Some Mahamudra texts read:

Rest with your meditation heightened like the sky and as expansive
as the earth.

And:

Rest within the uncontrived natural state, an equipoise that is
beyond all effort, like a great garuda gliding through the sky.

Meditate like the sun uncovered by clouds, brilliant and lucid.

If you are able to meditate with your mind released into evenness, heightened and spread out like the sky, you'll come to experience an utterly open, all-pervading expanse. This is the nature of mind. You must settle into this state. As Milarepa told the young girl Paldar Bum:

Meditate without center or boundary, as in the example of the sky.

Pema Karpo said:

Just like a great garuda soars in the sky, meditate in an honest and straightforward way, Pema Kar!

"Within meditation, an experience, a view like a vast, panoramic view of the sky seen from a high elevation—limpid, clear, naked, fresh, and totally open—will arise; remain in this great meditation, within an equipoise that is like the sky. This is nothing other than the essentially empty nature of the mind.

"At this time, it is imperative to recognize if there is a slight attitude, a thought identifying with and focusing upon the experience, lurking within a dark corner of your mind.

"If you have looked carefully and can't find any such thought, you have passed beyond objects into an experience that is utterly inexpressible. At this time, there is no need to analyze further; simply rest within the meditative absorption. The great luminous emptiness, devoid of any notion of 'this is it' is a vivid experience that is, nevertheless, utterly inexpressible. As it is said:

The perfection of wisdom is inconceivable and inexpressible, like the essence of the sky; it is beyond both birth and cessation.[1]

And:

I have found nectar-like Dharma: profound, peaceful, simple, luminous, and uncompounded. If I explain it, no one will understand; far better I remain in the forest.[2]

"When you are experiencing this, nonrecognition is the supreme recognition. To be without a point of reference is the supreme reference point. To continually remain within this state is the real practice.

"Should you fail to recognize this great wisdom—the essence of mind, naked, luminous emptiness—you'll simply be resting in a state of nonthought and confusing this with actual meditation. Should this occur, when the natural radiance of mind itself dawns, say from the accumulation of merit, purifying of negativities, receiving the guru's blessing, and so on, you may fail to recognize it and simply fall into and become lost in vague and ordinary states of indifference. Should this happen, whatever your meditation practice might be, you'll find it beset with, and difficult to separate from, this indistinct mental torpor.

"If you are unable to distinguish these two, the nature of mind and mental torpor, you may well waste your life in an experience of vague oblivion.

"The guru has many methods with which to directly point out the nature of mind, but the disciple has to be receptive to the instruction, to follow it, and above all meditate on it."

Lhaje Chogyal once again had an experience of the natural state, and he offered me a little song:

> The pith instructions of Madhyamaka, Mahamudra, and Dzogchen
> abide in the heart of their teacher—the ever-kind guru.
>
> While remaining within calm abiding, I analyze, using reasoning
> and scripture,
> And come to realize how everything is naturally sky-like.
> Whenever thoughts arise, I look at their nature, and without
> grasping,
> They are effortlessly liberated in the expanse.
>
> Awareness, the viewer itself, when looking for its own essence, can
> find nothing but emptiness.
> The viewer and its object are both purified in emptiness.
> There is nothing to "see" and all appears as if a drama.
>
> To relax, I leave everything just as it is and enjoy the show.
> An open, spacious, all-pervasive experience is thereby induced,
> A sky-like equipoise within which I understand all to be an
> indivisible mixture of appearance and mind.

Watching this appearing yet empty, spectacle of illusion,
There is no danger of falling into the deep chasm of the erroneous
    views of permanence and nihilism.
Having entered the great road of the spacious union,
I have no doubt as to the destination.

Having passed into the Dharmakaya Palace of Simplicity,
There is no room for elaboration.
Indeed, there isn't even much to be said,
For all is simply left and finally released within that which is
    inconceivable and inexpressible.

This little child of awareness, singing his little song, finds comfort in
    the all-pervasive dharmadhatu of his mother's lap.

It seems Lhaje Chogyal previously had problems enhancing his practice
of meditation and had harbored a lot of doubt. With this instruction I was
able to remove both of his obstacles. He later told me that he went on to have
an extraordinary experience of insight meditation.

"Removing all superimpositions concerning the natural state is a great
way to enhance genuine practice," he said.

# 20

# BUDDHAHOOD WITHOUT MEDITATION

---

My fortunate students the Lama of Ponmo Cave—the highly realized yogin Sonam Chopel—Tenzin Repa, Tenzin Gyurme, and Zopa Chopel came to visit. They said, "The teachings of Buddha are manifold, and their commentaries are too numerous to count! In these decadent times, life is short, and no one knows when they will pass away. We are all quite old and would like a fitting teaching, one that doesn't require a lot of effort-based meditation, but rather affords the practitioner great results with very little effort: instructions so excellent and profound that they cause buddhahood without meditation, and that render what is hidden in your heart fully evident, the mere hearing of which has the potential to rip the fabric of samsara to shreds." They went on:

> Yogi, you are like the full moon,
> Filled with the qualities of learning and realization.
> Your compassionate light pervades every direction and causes the
>     clusters of your water lily–like disciples to bloom.
>
> Yogi, you are like the best of captains,
> Having crossed the seas of worldly ties, you found gems of the divine
>     Dharma,
> Which you now explain to the satisfaction of all.
>
> Yogi, you are like a dharma king,
> Having fallen into the hands of the enemy, emotion and karma, you
>     cut all suffering,
> And the torments themselves were liberated as they beheld your face
>     and heard your words.

As for us, we find ourselves locked within the prison of samsara,
  bound tightly in the shackles of self-grasping.
Pierced and slashed by the weapons of afflictive emotion and
  karma,
We nurse the gaping wounds of sickness, aging, success, failure,
  and so on.

The messengers of days, months, and years drive us on,
And we are terrified as we come into the presence of the cruelest of
  judges, the Lord of Death.
When shall we arrive? Tonight? The next day?

We have come before you, O king of the Dharma—
Both skilled and of great influence—
To ask you to lift the bondage of samsara's prison a little, and grant
  us the fortune of liberation.
Dharmaraja, be kind we pray!
In return, we'll offer you our wholehearted practice.

As prisoners, we continually seek your refuge; as disciples, we four
  hereby make a request:

The teaching of Buddha is vast indeed and commentaries thereupon,
  myriad.
In this decadent age, life is short, and the hour of death's arrival
  unknown.

In your great love, pray pour your nectar-like instruction—
A veritable panacea, the mere taste of which alleviates the disease of
  afflictive emotions—
Into the golden vessel of your faithful students.

I replied:

The three jewels are our constant and unmistaken refuge,
While the three roots bestow inexhaustible accomplishment,
And the dharma guardians accomplish our activity without
  impediment.

These, however, are all a magical manifestation of unborn mind.
Once realized, the precious nature of mind is the only refuge we
  need;
With single-pointed devotion, I pay homage to it from the very
  depths of my heart.

You fortunate ones who desire buddhahood in this lifetime,
Listen with devotion as I explain a most sublime instruction.

"Furthermore, within the expanse of the vast sky that is free of center and border, the sun journeys freely, illuminating all four continents. Similarly, the renown of the completely unrivaled monarch of the realized ones of ancient India, the magnificent Saraha, has crossed the very borders of existence and illuminates the very reaches of space. This is his vajra song, a doha, taken from the fine vase of his speech:

Mind is the source of all; samsara and nirvana both emanate from it,
And it can provide any result you might desire.
Pay homage to mind—a wish-fulfilling gem![1]

"To elucidate this lion's roar of a verse just a little and put it into context with the ground, path, and result of practice:"

## GROUND

**Mind is the source of all;**

"**Mind** is like the sky, empty without border or center; it pervades absolutely everything, yet is itself without direction or division. It cannot be defined as this or that but is an utterly open, all-pervasive expanse of emptiness and luminosity, which is impossible to grasp and beyond any elaboration. It **is the source** or origin **of all** phenomena, both animate and inanimate, that are included within samsara and nirvana—the environment, beings, your own body, and so on. Everything has the natural state of mind, the all-pervasive, ungraspable, vast expanse of luminous emptiness, as its root. Failure to recognize this is called ignorance.

"This ignorance causes us to grasp on to an independent 'I,' which in turn causes a dichotomy into self and others, leading to attachment and aversion, and from there the eighty-four thousand destructive emotions arise and proliferate. They in turn lead to action, karma, both positive and negative, and this brings about the myriad confused appearances of pleasure and pain—none of which are true, but which, nevertheless, are grasped at as being so. Samsara has existed since time without beginning. It is the continual perpetuation of illusory, dreamlike appearances within which all manner of experience, either pleasant or otherwise, can be had.

"To thoroughly eliminate the root of samsara, the ignorance that is a lack of realization of the natural state, you'll need to know well the ways of meditation that are a path to its removal, and, having cleansed ignorance, you need to know the ways of awakening."

## PATH

**samsara and nirvana both emanate from it,**

"The guru who reveals this path to you should be extremely well qualified and sublime, such that you should want to take the dust from his feet and place it on the crown of your head. You must take the crucial points of his oral instructions to heart and realize the nature of your mind—the ground of **both samsara and nirvana.**

"At the moment, we find everything obscured by the adventitious defilements of ignorance, afflictive emotion, and karma. These, in turn, emanate everything that appears and exists within samsara.

"Ignorance causes the confused appearance of a truly existing, self-identity. Such an identity doesn't exist yet is grasped at and held as being real. This addiction has prevailed since time without beginning and has caused us to wander aimlessly in samsara.

"Having realized this grasping to be mistaken, it is imperative to cease falling under its influence. Using numerous quotations and lines of reasoning, a certainty that everything within samsara and nirvana **emanates from** and is none other than the display of mind—appearing yet empty, like a dream or an illusion—must be reached, for this will serve as your path.

"Investigate the nature of mind, that which serves as the basis of both samsara and nirvana. You'll find it essentially and primordially empty yet luminous; ungraspable, it is an open, all-pervasive expanse—like the sky. To realize this in meditation is sky-like equipoise, and you should strive to remain in this both day and night for months or years.

"At this time, you shouldn't seek to invite thoughts, be they good, bad, and so on, or follow them. Neither encouraging nor rejecting thought, give up all mental exertion. Simply sustain the great, all-pervasive, uncontrived nature of mind.

"There is no need for so much as a hair's tip of an effort-based antidote to gross and subtle concepts and thought. Simply release all of them as they arise, and adventitious obscurations, afflictive emotions, karma, and so on, will all be purified in their own ground.

"Having seized the citadel of the great dharmakaya—the carefree expanse of naked, empty luminosity that lies beyond the ordinary mind—your realization will be unchanging, like space, and the qualities of nirvana will unfold and be fully internalized.

"To sustain this natural state is the unmistaken path. Having taken hold of the instruction, it is crucial that you put it into practice."

## RESULT

**And it can provide any result you might desire.**

"As the temporary aims of both self and other are met through the force of practice, this instruction on mind **can provide** any desired **result**. Ultimately it reveals the sky-like enlightened intent, the unborn mind that is beyond all elaboration—the dharmakaya. Without moving from this realization, the two rupakayas appear clearly and individually, like rainbows in the sky, and altogether they give rise to the results that both **you** and others **desire**.

**Pay homage to mind—a wish-fulfilling gem!**

"As all desired effects are thereby won, this precious **mind** of ultimate bodhichitta is likened to **a wish-fulfilling gem** and Saraha concludes his verse with this simile in a line of **homage.**

"From within a multitude of sublime instructions coming from supreme masters, this is the most sublime and wondrous path. To be inseparable from the realization of appearance and mind is to be never separated from method and wisdom. Other than this, you needn't seek any other method and wisdom.

"All the effort-based practices of method and wisdom, such as those found in the paths of creation and completion and other 'lower' spiritual approaches are included within this wondrous practice—a great wide-open and carefree path, the union of appearance and mind.

"There are those who harbor doubt; they wonder if this most excellent path of conjoined method and wisdom were to become one-sided, wouldn't it be mistaken? It would. However, this is the path of conjoined method and wisdom, where mind and the phenomena of both samsara and nirvana are conjoined and carried within a sole path of method and wisdom. As such, there is no need for such doubt.

"Just as the untethered snow lion leaps through snowy ranges, the unrivaled and mighty yogi Mila Shepa Dorje awakened to buddhahood in a single lifetime. He is renowned in both celestial and human realms, where it is said that he is spoken about more than a hundred times a day. He once sang:

> Having great uncertainty, I sought an authentic path—
> The open path of the union of appearance and emptiness—
> Having practiced it, I no longer have any doubt!

"The essentially and primordially empty, sky-like nature of all phenomena within samsara and nirvana is realized through the profound instructions of sublime masters; it aspect appears like a ceaseless dream. Dreams appear from mind; they also appear to mind. Similarly, sights, sounds, everything in fact, is empty, yet still appears—emerging from mind and appearing to mind. Even things considered being 'over there.'

"The nature of mind is the source of everything—its root and ground. Yet it wasn't produced by anyone or anything, nor does it have cause or condition. It is primordially empty, like the sky—free from direction and partiality, an all-pervading emptiness that cannot be pointed to or characterized—the great dharmadhatu; utterly open, it is an expanse free of every extreme.

"Having realized the emptiness of mind, all sights and sounds appear unceasingly within it like reflections in a mirror. Do not try to prevent them from appearing, but make sure they are not grasped at. Within mind itself—the completely open, ungraspable, empty luminosity—experience the objects of the five senses without restriction.

"Rest in the great expanse of sky-like emptiness that lies beyond all extremes and is free of duality. Through single-pointed meditation, appearances and mind will mix to become of one taste within the great expanse of meditative equipoise.

"This isn't a one-sided equipoise; appearances are not left outside, as if existing in and of themselves, and mind itself isn't lost inside. Wherever there are appearances, you will find them pervaded by emptiness, the sky-like equipoise, which is itself infinitely pervaded by appearances.

"Things appear while remaining essentially empty and while empty, things continue to appear unceasingly. This union of appearance and emptiness is vaster than the sky; it is the unmistaken path taken by all buddhas across the three times. *The Five Stages* says:

> Where there is freedom from the concept of samsara and nirvana—
>    everything is one;
> It is explained as the union.

And:

> When the relative and ultimate are seen as aspects of one another,
> They integrate perfectly and are thus explained to be a union.

"Just as a wish-fulfilling jewel is the source of all that is desired, practice of this most spacious path, the union of appearance and emptiness, method and wisdom, is the source for the effortless acquisition of Buddha's qualities. The foremost venerable Milarepa said:

> Existence, the appearance of things,
> And the nonexistence of things, their empty suchness, are essentially
>    indivisible—of one taste.
> In this equipoise, the terms 'awareness of self' and 'awareness of
>    other' do not exist;
> Everything is the spacious union.

> Whoever realizes this is truly learned.
> It isn't seen by consciousness, but rather by wisdom.
> It isn't seen by sentient beings, but rather by buddhas.
> It isn't seen by a subjective consciousness, but rather by reality itself.

> Like requests made to a precious wish-fulfilling gem,
> Compassion spontaneously wells forth from this realization,

As do the qualities of Buddha such as the powers[2] and the retention
   that doesn't forget.
This is my, a yogin's, measure of realization.

You gods and demons gathered here, I have spoken the profound
   Dharma,
Yet you prefer the sounds of Bon.
In the kingdom of Abarahi, even the learned must listen to the
   whims of the insane, But when the lion roars, even the foxes and
   wolves at home in their cemeteries quiver in fear.
There may yet be a few of you who have the fortune to achieve
   liberation through hearing my song.

Rechungpa said:

Desire to know the one thing that liberates all.

Repa Shiwa O said:

The instruction of a single word to place you in buddhahood . . .

"These quotes all refer to this oral instruction, one that brings together
all the practice instructions of the sutras and tantras. The lordly Mila said:

Appearances are mind and mind itself is emptiness.
To be continually within this realization and experience, ethics,
   offering, and all other virtuous actions are naturally included.

*The Ear-Whispered Tradition of the Dakini Chakrasambhava* states:[3]

Meditate upon the one instruction that illustrates them all.
Similarly, achieve one ground while simultaneously winning them
   all—
And win all instructions through receiving this one direct
   transmission.

*The Tantra That Causes Liberation through Contact* says:

The paths and grounds of all the various spiritual approaches are contained within the one ground of pure self-awareness.

A sutra says:

I have given various teachings throughout the various realms of the world. The words may differ, but the meaning is one; to meditate well on that one word is akin to meditating on them all.

*The Perfection of Wisdom* states:

To know the one dharma, a sutra and its explanation, well is to know all dharmas.

The Madhyamikas say:

Whoever sees one thing is said to see all;
The emptiness of one thing is the emptiness of all.[4]

"I have thought about these and many other such quotations, and they all point to the same thing, awakening to the unborn nature of mind—the vast dharmadhatu—the ultimate and most crucial point of the entire eighty-four thousand bundles of Dharma. The Lordly Dorje Gyalpo wrote:[5]

When you have seen the crucial point,
The moisture of words may gather in clouds,
But inevitably falls to the ground of the unborn.[6]

The peerless Atisha said:

The eighty-four thousand heaps of Dharma discourse all lead to suchness.

"As such, should you desire to awaken to buddhahood in a single lifetime, you have the instructions in the palm of your hand! As Marpa of Lodrak said to Milarepa:

If you desire to awaken in a single lifetime, watch your mind without
distraction!

Similarly, Atisha said:

Drom, as you desire to awaken quickly, I'll teach you the profound
secret mantra.

There is nothing closer to buddhahood than the practice of the dohas, the
practice instructions of the great mahasiddhas. As it is said, when autumn
is upon us and the harvest ripe, it's almost time to eat! To practice them will
cause great realization, to the delight of all.

"Those of greater acumen should practice the higher Dharma. Your
actions are in accord with that acumen, and I have taught you this song.
Not only is it the highest teaching of the secret mantra vehicle, it is a most
profound doha; through it, I received the blessings of Saraha. I now share it
with you—keep it well, in the very depths of your heart.

"A man rests in his home after the hard work of gathering in the harvest.
Similarly, after the hard work of the preliminaries and coming to an understanding of the Dharma, a yogin with absolute certainty in the ungraspable empty luminosity that is the nature of mind—the great dharmadhatu
beyond all elaboration—need no longer burden himself with deity yoga,
mantra recitation, and so on. Giving up all such elaborate, effort-based practices, he need only remain in sky-like meditative equipoise. The wish to do
anything else is simply an impediment. *The Secret Accomplishment* states:

A master who tells you the vajra-mind of awakening and so on is
won only through mudras, mandalas, mantras, and such like, is
none other than a demon!

Milarepa said:

While meditating upon Mahamudra, give up both physical and
verbal virtue,
For there is every danger it'll distract you from nonconceptual
wisdom.
My child, simply rest within the uncontrived state!

"Abandoning such genuine wisdom to engage in lesser virtue would be akin to a king giving up his throne to sweep floors. As the glorious Saraha sang:

> Having realized the natural state of mind only to leave it for other, lesser virtues is to be like a king abdicating his throne to become a cleaner;
> Giving up inexhaustible great bliss only to become ensnared in the gross, physical bliss of the world.

"Having eaten your fill, there is no need to look for more to eat is there? Similarly, having resolved the nature of mind, there is no need to learn other subjects such as the sciences, and so on. To sustain this realization alone is sufficient. The Lordly Sana Ratna said:

> The supreme state is won through the single-pointed pursuit of meditation;
> Herein accomplishment is found.
> Nothing is gained through constant distraction.

"Having realized the nature of mind that lies beyond any and all elaboration and to then make a great effort to learn many 'other' things is, as it is said, like

> having found a precious jewel, to continue to search for semiprecious stones, or to leave a fine meal to go in search of junk food!

"There is no need to mention the necessity of giving up 'outer' worldly actions. However, while resting in meditative, sky-like equipoise, it is also imperative to lay 'inner distractions' such as charity and making offerings to one side. Buddhakara said:[7]

> A yogin who wishes to familiarize himself with wisdom doesn't wander around too much; neither does he eat too much, speak a lot, shout, practice asana, recite scriptures, make offerings, perform fire rituals, and so forth, rather he gives them up. Their abandonment is samadhi.

"Saraha said that to leave the nectar-like instructions of your guru and go in search of other instructions is like leaving a source of water to wander in deserts and die of thirst:

> He who leaves the nectar-like instructions of his guru, not using them to quench his thirst and cool the torments of mind, and needlessly goes in search of other teachings, suffers greatly in that pursuit; he like a person who leaves a water source to wander in deserts and dies of thirst there.
>
> A deer seeks out a place to sleep soundly among snow and glacier, rocks and crags in the uninhabited higher grounds of mountains and valleys. Having found such a place, he makes it his own and continually returns to it. Similarly, a yogin seeks out solitude and places his body, speech, and mind in an unmoving absorption that runs smoothly like a steady river, continuously, like water in a strong fall, and well bound, like the tip of a lamp's wick. Similarly, a yogin rests in stable meditative equipoise throughout day and night.
>
> Give up restlessness, distraction, feelings, and desires of acquiring the slight accomplishments of the world, such as the ability to repel external forces, the eight accomplishments, and so on.[8]

"Meditate single-pointedly on the nonconceptual wisdom of Mahamudra, the great accomplishment, and a yogin with either great diligence or training in a past life will obtain the supreme accomplishment within six months. *The Summary of Conduct* reads:

> Accomplishment will be won within six months.

"This is a meditation technique that doesn't require great effort, and so on; it is an instruction for gaining buddhahood without meditation, if you have such an instruction. Marpa said:

> Everyone has meditation instructions with which to achieve buddhahood, but to achieve it without meditation is enlightened indeed!

"Such instruction should be kept from those who insist that effort-based meditation is necessary for enlightenment and also from those who have a different, a lower or lesser, disposition to practice. This is not to prevent faults from being found in the instruction, far from it! It is rather to protect those who wouldn't appreciate or understand the instruction from creating wrong views toward it, ridiculing and abandoning it, thereby creating the extremely negative action of rejecting the Dharma. As such, keep it well hidden. *The Reverberation of Sound Tantra* reads:

> If this mode of simply resting in the natural state is explained to those who are suited toward the spiritual approaches of hearers and solitary realizers, they will become terrified and pass out. As such it is imperative that it be kept secret.

*The Heap of Jewels Tantra* goes on to say:

> Do not breathe so much as a word of these instructions to those who favor the spiritual approach of the hearers and solitary realizers. Why? Well, should they hear it, they will immediately become scared, terror will grip their hearts, and they will inevitably pass out. Showing no respect for and ridiculing secret mantra, they become anxious, and inevitably, when that karma ripens, they will experience the great hells. What need is there to mention teaching the subject to such individuals, it shouldn't even be taught downwind of them!

Such instruction is like a wish-fulfilling jewel. The sublime Atisha and Lobsang Drakpa, along with their followers, kept this instruction extremely hidden. Don't think they didn't possess it just because they didn't advertise it!

> The garuda-like siddhas of old, spread wide their wings of
> appearance and emptiness conjoined.
> Soaring high into the vast expanse of omniscience, the lofty peaks of
> the three worlds are left far behind.

"We, their fortunate baby garuda-like disciples, have broken out of the shell of the eight worldly concerns and, wishing to follow our parents, should retreat to isolated caves, spread wide our fully matured wings of the union, and fly after them."

My disciple Tenzin Repa asked, "Your instruction is extremely beneficial to us. Tell me; when sustaining the natural state, are thoughts and concepts taken onto the path or not?"

I replied, "When waves arise from an ocean, they do not change it; the ocean remains the same. Waves, no matter how big they might be, are unable to stand on their own; merging back into the ocean, they inevitably vanish. Similarly, when resting, relaxed and serene, within the natural state of mind—the utterly open, all-pervading, and vast expanse of meditative equipoise—myriad thoughts, good, bad, and so on, may arise. If you simply remain unmoved in the natural state, of the many concepts, ideas, and thoughts that arise, not one of them is able to stand on its own. They will all inevitably dissolve back whence they came—into the expanse of the sky-like meditative equipoise. None will remain. A tantra reads:

> The waves that are a movement of mind,
> Like waves on an ocean,
> Dissolve back whence they came—
> The ocean of the primordial ground.

"Similarly, when you recognize that you are distracted, dull, or tired, simply return to the natural state of mind and these thoughts will be set free. There is no need to take concepts and thoughts as a separate path. If you remain in this realization, the equipoise itself will deal with them. As Milarepa sang:

> If you experience bliss in meditation,
> Simply recognize it as the magical display of mind and continue
> meditating within mind itself.

The Great Master of Oddiyana said:

> Whatever thoughts and emotions of the five poisons stir in your
> mind, do not welcome them, or chase them away.
> Allow them to settle without the slightest fabrication in the ground
> of their own arising, and they are immediately set free in the
> dharmakaya.[9]

When thoughts and emotions arise, don't ponder upon or grasp at them; there is also no need to think about blocking them. Whatever thoughts arise, let them arise, but don't follow them. Allow thoughts to arise while remaining relaxed in the expanse of the previously established nature. Remaining in the natural state, the arising and liberation of thoughts will occur simultaneously.

"Be like a snow lion, unfazed by a snowfall, an elephant unmoved by a thorn, and an empty house within which a thieving dog has nothing to gain and the landlord nothing to lose. As the vidyadhara Shri Singha said:

> Nonarising, nonarising, arise, arise, arisen—don't grasp!
> The arising and liberation of thoughts will occur
> simultaneously.[10]

"Another example used is that of a snake unknotting itself. The snake doesn't need to rely upon another to untangle himself; he manages it alone. Similarly, by remaining within mind itself, whatever thought or concept arises, it is immediately liberated in its own ground without the slightest need for an antidote. A tantra reads:

> Whatever arises is released within awareness, like a snake untying
> itself.

"The sky remains unmoved whichever way the wind may blow: north, south, east, or west, and the wind doesn't obscure the sky. Birds of all sizes fly within its depths and leave no trace; they likewise cannot affect it. Similarly, while remaining in sky-like meditative equipoise, whatever thoughts may arise, don't grasp at them; simply remain in the meditation. Concepts and thoughts cannot obscure it. None of the eighty-four thousand destructive emotions can affect it. Let thoughts arise, but do not grasp at them. This is taking thought as a path—where concepts and thoughts neither benefit nor harm and where it is impossible for meditation to get better or worse. The most crucial and sublime of instructions is to continually remain within the nature of mind. *The Heart Essence of the Dakini* states:

> Wherever you abide, remain within awareness.
> Whatever arises, it is simply the radiance of awareness—
> Vast and unchanging like the sky.

Essentially, to sustain the sky-like equipoise is to remain within the realization of suchness, emptiness. This is the greatest antidote to everything you wish to be free of: destructive emotions, thoughts, concepts, distractions, dullness, and sleepiness.

> You may carry many weapons of instruction taken from the sutras
> and tantras,
> But if you don't use them to subdue the enemy, the destructive
> emotions, what's the point?
> You need to be a warrior who wields the sharp weapon of the guru's
> pith instructions and uses it to smite the enemy of emotion!

> Disciples who like to wander in the plains of great bliss,
> Be sure to carry the sharp spear of the view with you.
> Should the enemy of emotion try to prevent you from entering the
> door to the citadel of mind, use it to slay him where he stands!"

Tenzin Gyurme went on to ask, "When meditating like this, is there a special need to develop compassion?"

I replied, "The root of everything is the nature of mind, the great dharmadhatu—empty luminosity that is utterly open and all-pervading. When you realize this and remain within the experience both day and night, you'll naturally give rise to an impartial and extraordinarily strong compassion for all parent sentient beings that haven't realized it. *The Abridged Empowerment* says:

> Boundless compassion is the fruit of the wish-fulfilling tree of
> emptiness.

Similarly:

> Once the strength of the bodhisattva's meditative equipoise is
> perfected through familiarity, the demon of fixation is done away
> with and, most importantly, genuine compassion is born.

The Indian Padampa said:

> Realization of emptiness and compassion arise together.

Je Dorje Gyalpo said:

When you no longer discriminate between an enemy who wants to see you dead and an ordinary fellow, you have mastered love and compassion.

"An accomplished yogin is one who works for the benefit of others within the realization of conjoined compassion and emptiness. The lordly Milarepa said:

> Genuine compassion is born when emptiness is realized.
> At this time, there is no distinction between self and other and the
>     welfare of others is naturally accomplished.

Such yogins are worthy objects of homage for all. As Longchen Rabjam has written:

> The faithful should place such fortunate ones, awareness holders
> gone to bliss, at their crowns and pay them homage. Bow before
> these sources of bliss that exceed the wish-fulfilling jewel and
> turn to them for refuge.

Shantideva wrote:[11]

> I bow to him in whom the sacred mind of bodhichitta is born;
> I take refuge in that source of joy who brings happiness even to those
>     who harm him."

To conclude, I sang:

> The sun of compassion shines without partiality in the vast, sky-like,
>     empty luminosity that is the nature of mind.
> Its radiance naturally clears away the illusory cloud banks of
>     destructive emotion gathering in the south and effortlessly cares
>     for all lotus-like beings.

> Marvelous indeed to so much as hear of this unprecedented yoga
>     that works tirelessly to sail across the ocean of samsara in a boat of
>     conjoined compassion and emptiness.

Finally, Zopa Chopel asked, "Are the dramas of samsara and nirvana seen when sustaining the natural state of mind?"

I answered, "Being extremely vast and spacious, it pervades both samsara and nirvana; being sky-like, extremely bright, vividly clear, and unobscured, it allows everything to arise within it; being as unflawed as a polished crystal mirror, the depths and reach of its reflections are difficult to fathom; it is free of any reference point, like a large body of water.

"The ultimate mind of bodhichitta lies beyond all elaboration; it is like the center of a very clear sky. It is an ungraspable empty luminosity—an utterly open, free, panoramic expanse. Occasionally, when resting in equipoise within this basic space, natural luminosity will separate from the dross of contrived meditation and will become vivid and clear.

"At times such as these, you may experience clear visions of places you've been to, your homeland, and so on, or of places you have never been to before, such as China or India. You may see people you know such as your parents; you may also see gods and demons, and so forth. You may gradually come to clearly perceive the buddhas and bodhisattvas dwelling in the pure buddha realms of the ten directions and also the myriad phenomena of samsara and nirvana.

"Previously, while resting in meditation, Lord Milarepa saw Rechungpa's movements and travels in India. He also saw the route he would take upon his return to Tibet and went to meet him.

"Similarly, once, during his meditation, Rechungpa had a vision of the whole of existence, from its root right up to the pinnacle. At the time, he wondered what his master, Milarepa, was up to and saw him teaching a few disciples at the Dropa Cave in Nyanang. Milarepa knew exactly what Rechungpa was experiencing and exclaimed, 'My child Rechungpa has been driven insane by the demon of Mahamudra practice!'

"Mila also said, 'The eyes of the world are shortsighted indeed; even with my head covered, I can see further than they can!' And:

Of what use are the limitless visions that arise in mind?

"As such, it is imperative to continually watch your mind. Should you wish to watch the wondrous visions that arise, do so; but do not grasp at them! If you remain continually free of attachment and grasping, the time will come when everything in both samsara and nirvana will be realized as perfect within your mind; you will have accomplished the permanent domain of the dharmakaya within your own mind and completed your spiritual journey. Milarepa said:

> Gods gathered here, know that the supreme instruction is to see you own mind as the dharmakaya. If you do that, you will have brought your spiritual activities to their natural conclusion and you'll be able to see all the various dramas within samsara and nirvana."

I sang:

> While relaxing within the dharmadhatu's all-pervading expanse,
>     I am at ease and free of all care! Let me sing you a little song:
>
> Should you wish to view samsara and nirvana as a drama,
> Don't bother looking at many things; simply look at your mind.
> Look! Does it have an origin, a dwelling, or a destination?
> Look! Are the three stillness, movement, and awareness empty or
>     not?
> Look! Is emptiness possible to grasp?
> If not, look again! Does it have a center or periphery?
>
> Mind itself, free of middle and boundary, is as vast as space.
> Utterly transparent, both inside and out, it is free of all borders and
>     direction.
>
> I realize the nature of this all-pervasive and open mind that has
>     neither center nor periphery—like space.
> It has neither an increase nor a decrease of radiance—like the sun
>     and moon,
> And that is ungraspable—like the sky.
> Essentially, everything arises within this mind!
> May this little song of mine prove meaningful!

After I sang a few more songs and provided them a little counsel, my four disciples became extremely happy. Rejoicing greatly, they offered me many prostrations and returned to their hermitages where they diligently applied themselves to single-pointed meditation on the natural state.

# 21

# How to Prepare for, Practice in, and Gain Accomplishment in the Various In-between Bardo States

My two fortunate disciples Lobsang Jinpa and Tenzin Gyatso offered me a flawless silk scarf along with a request for instructions on the ways to achieve liberation at the time of death, in the bardo, and for the means to travel to the pure realms. They went on:

> Emanation of Buddha, my lordly master and guru, having spent your
>    entire youth serving many gurus, you received much instruction.
>
> Later, you exerted yourself in practice and diligently applied yourself
>    to meditation in lonely places.
> The signs and qualities of genuine practice arose and before too long
>    you actualized the three kayas.
>
> Finally, at this, the time of your resultant accomplishment,
> You have directed many fortunate disciples, headed by those of this
>    region, to higher states of rebirth and the definitive excellence of
>    enlightenment.
>
> The specifics of your outer, inner, and secret life of liberation are too
>    numerous to mention,
> As such, please know that we pay homage at your lotus feet, not just
>    once, but time and time again!
>
> Precious guru, we vajra brothers, the most wretched among your
>    disciples, would like to make a single request:
> You know that we are dull of mind and bereft of practice.
> Youth is spent; we are aged and close to death.

Too great an explanation would be lost on us,
And whatever we do manage to pick up, we'll find it hard to find the
time to meditate upon; accordingly, look kindly upon us.

Previously, you have expounded, in great detail and on many
occasions, the wondrous instructions of Madhyamaka,
Mahamudra, Dzogchen, Chöd, and so on,
Profound and far-reaching instructions, all.
Delightful to hear, their sound alone brings great joy to the mind.

For the sake of us dimwits, kindly extract a brief synopsis: the
liberating view of natural luminosity, the method of the creation
phase,
For liberation in the intermediate state, and of the ways to purify
samsara's realms and proceed to a pure land—
Something we can actually remember and apply!

When unsure of things, we supplicate you.
In your great love and concern,
Pray grant us extremely clear instruction—
One that will allow us to think of death with ease.

There is no greater refuge than you.
Please hold the two of us in your compassion.
May we never be parted—
Not here, in the bardo, not at anytime!

When we come to die, may we come into your presence, O protector,
and receive guidance to the dharmakaya.
Failing to achieve liberation by experiencing death as the dharmakaya,
May we transform the appearances of the intermediate state into
friendly sambhogakayas.
And should that fail, pray lead us to pure lands such as Manifest Joy
in the east!

I replied, "You two of fortune should know the instructions you seek are
all included in the previous instructions that I gave. I'll summarize them
for you in mnemonic verse:

Grounded in faith and possessed of ethics,
You are good-natured and you are kind.
Disciples of mine, Lobsang Jinpa and Tenzin Gyatso, lend me your
    ear as I, Tsogdruk Rangdrol, a yogin, sing you a little song that
    will prove most useful;
A ditty worth more than a thousand measures of gold!

Life is short and the time of death unknown,
After death we must go on, that much we do know.

To be liberated in the dharmakaya at death,
Remain within the view of the natural state.

To be liberated as the sambhogakaya during the bardo,
Meditate on the creation phase—
The appearing yet empty form of the deity.

To be born in pure lands, continually purify yourself and reveal the
    realms of the five families.

If you practice like this, when death comes, you'll be prepared and
    know what to do."

Jinpa then said, "Many thanks for those concise mnemonic lines. The
two of us are, as you know, very dull and forgetful. The lines you gave us are
perhaps too short and we might find it hard to recall their meaning. May
I ask you to elucidate a little further, please?"
To which I replied:

The essence of everything is primordially empty, and from within
    that emptiness, appearances arise like dreams,
And just as those dreams appear from mind, so too do all
    phenomena.

The fundamental nature of mind is primordially beyond grasping.
It is a union of emptiness and lucidity, vast like the sky.
This is the dharmadhatu, free of all peripheries.
Let go and relax within this expanse.

Clouds may well gather in the vast sky,
But when the wind blows, they scatter.
Similarly, when torpor, dullness, and drowsiness gather, your
     awareness can be made clearer through the raising of your gaze.
May awareness be realized as a carefree, all-pervading expanse, a vast
     and lofty expanse, like the sky.

With torpor, dullness, and drowsiness purified in their own ground,
Meditation is brilliant and as unobscured as space.

As waves arise from the ocean,
So too thoughts from the mind.
When oceans still, their waves are pacified.
Within the stillness of equipoise upon the empty clarity of mind
     itself, thoughts similarly calm.

Meditative equipoise within the natural state,
Thoughts and concepts naturally released within their own space,
And holding the ground of the natural state,
These three, although spoken of separately, are to be practiced
     together, as one.

Meditating like this, you'll master the finest equipoise;
And when you die, you'll surely be liberated in the dharmakaya.

Tenzin Gyatso thanked me. He went on to request a similar explanation
for the visualizations of the creation phase practice. I replied:

Dissolve yourself, your environment, and all beings within
     emptiness.
Within that emptiness, appearing instantaneously like reflections in
     a mirror, the elements appear one upon the other;
The inestimable mansion sits atop them all.

At its center, you appear as the yidam deity.
You must appear clearly, with the stable pride of being the deity.
Meditate on lights and offering goddesses radiating from the seed-
     syllable and the surrounding mantra garland at your heart.

They make offerings to the buddhas and bodhisattvas and return
with their blessings in the form of lights.
These lights dissolve into you and purify your negativities and
obscurations.
You become one with the deity and possess its power.

Light is radiated once again, it permeates the entire universe and its
inhabitants, cleansing them of impurity, fault, and defect.
Have the strong belief that the entire environment arises as the
mandala of the deity and all sentient beings as deities—
Every sound is mantra and conceptual thought is wisdom.
Recite the mantra of sound and emptiness conjoined.

To conclude, absorb everything within emptiness.
And, from within that emptiness, arise as the deity to make your
prayers of auspiciousness and dedication.

If you are able to meditate accordingly and are not liberated within
the dharmakaya at the time of death,
Your deity yoga will surely purify the mental body of the
intermediate state and you'll be liberated as the sambhogakaya.

Jinpa told me my explanation, though brief, was easy to comprehend. He
asked me to view them both with compassion and to offer a similar explanation of the methods to purify the various realms of samsara. I replied:

Having entered the path of natural luminosity, the gurus, yidams,
and dakinis will gradually guide you to the pure realms of the five
buddha families such as Manifest Joy.

Please all the buddhas who dwell there by making offerings and
prostrations.
Then raise a hand to your ear and listen to the beautiful melodious
tunes;
Have no doubt, they will prophesy your enlightenment.

One day you will die; if, at that time, you think that you would
like to travel to a pure realm, it is necessary to complement those
thoughts with prayer.

To that end, if you purify your life yet do not liberate as a
   sambhogakaya in the bardo,
Keep the intention to be born in a nirmanakaya pure land in mind,
And it is certain that you'll be miraculously born from a lotus in
   whichever realm you contemplate.

Listen to the teachings of the Buddha and practice them well,
For once you awaken yourself, it will then be up to you to serve as
   guide for those still sleeping in impure realms.

"We have both created negative karma," they said. "Not only that but we
are greatly obscured by the karmic consequence of having misappropriated
offerings made to the sangha. If we lack the fortune to travel to such pure
realms, what should we do?" they asked.

I replied, "Due to your past actions, if you are unable to travel to the
pure realms, understand that during the time of the intermediate state, you
will be possessed of clairvoyance and other miraculous powers. The highly
realized adepts of India and Tibet instructed us that we should use them to
seek out future parents who are of high status and sympathetic toward the
Dharma. Having found such parents, visualize them as Vajradhara in union
with his consort and the womb of your future mother as a celestial mansion.
To project your consciousness into its middle, meditate upon yourself as a
tiny syllable HUNG and make the following prayers of aspiration:

Through the blessing of the gurus, the might of the merit of the
three times gathered by myself and all others, may I, through
the support of these parents, obtain a human form replete with
the freedoms and endowments. May I become just like Mila
Shepa Dorje, who, through his sincere practice of the Dharma,
achieved perfect awakening in one lifetime and completely fulfilled the benefit of others.

"While strongly making these aspirations and visualizations, imagine
that your mind, in the form of a HUNG syllable, enters into the celestial
mansion. At this moment, the intermediate state will cease and conception
will have occurred. You will have secured a precious human body in dependence upon which you'll be able to achieve buddhahood in a single lifetime."

The two of them were greatly pleased. The offered me prostrations and
thanked me profusely before returning to their little dwellings.

# 22

# THE BENEFIT OF RETREAT

My disciple Wongpo, a local chief, one who is rich with the jewels of the aryas, asked me to tell him the benefit of dwelling in lonely mountainous retreats. He went on:

> Recollection of impermanence and the drawbacks of samsara,
> Coupled with the understanding that all beings have been my parents,
> Has led me to strongly desire to become Buddha—for the benefit of both all others and myself.

> To this effect, I have relied upon a qualified guru and received and contemplated his vast and profound teachings.
> Now to cut the fetters of this life and live up to the reputation of a hermit!

> Youthful white clouds gather around the mountain's peak, while silvery mist gathers at its waist.
> A mother deer and her fawn dance joyfully upon the grassy meadows that lie beautified with flowers, at the foot.
> Bees busily buzz their songs, and birds happily dive and soar.

> In joyous places such as these, pleasure groves of isolated mountain solitude, awareness is clear.
> You can live alone like the rishis of old,
> Meditate on the profound and vast teachings,
> And actualize the twofold benefit of self and other in this very life.

> Perfect guru, most precious, pray grant those of us who seek to emulate you, your praises of isolated places such as these.

Bless us that we might follow your example and dwell in
mountainous retreats, practice well, and awaken in exact accord
with the Dharma.

I replied, "The compounded, mundane phenomena of samsara appear as
if a drama, or the celestial cities of gandharvas. Reflecting on their changing,
impermanent, and momentary nature causes a great sadness. In particular,
the three cyclic worlds are, in and of themselves, the nature of suffering;
you'll not find a needle tip's worth of enduring happiness there. Recognizing
this will cause revulsion and renunciation to naturally arise within you in
such a way that you'll never forget them.

"This, in turn, will inspire you to seek out and roam in isolated hills,
valleys, and forests with a resolve that would remain unmoved should you
be offered even the pleasure grove of a sovereign monarch covered in a lat-
ticework of the finest jewels, or enticed with promises of beautiful houses,
high thrones, the finest silken clothes to wear, and the best teas and finest
wines with which to pass the time.

"Having partaken of the teachings, the desires and rejections of the eight
worldly concerns are enough to make you sick to your stomach.[1]

"Completely reject any notion or clinging to the idea of anything as
real, and wishes for the pleasures of samsara will not arise—not even for a
moment.

"Just as when, for example, a man is caught in the midday sun, he will
inevitably be tormented and parched. He will desperately seek water to
quench his thirst, and once found, he will drink his fill.

"Similarly, having thought long and hard about birth, death, and the
faults of samsara, mental anguish consumes the contemplative. It leads him
to desperately seek a qualified guru. Having found one, he will immediately
quench his torment with the continual study and contemplation of the vast
and profound nectar of the oral instructions. Satisfied, he will strive hard to
achieve complete and perfect buddhahood for the sake of all pitiful, parent
sentient beings.

"To this effect, a contemplative will seek out mountains whose peaks
are ornamented in youthful white clouds, where the sun rises early in the
morning and sets long into the evening—providing a long day full of light.
He will seek out a place of nature, of unspoiled beauty, where clear water
cascades down falls of white rock, offering cool refreshment, and groves
full of lovely sounds, where foliage and trees, beautified with flowers and
laden with fruit, are swayed by cool, scented breezes. If seen from afar, they

seem to move in great swaying motions, waving their branches as if calling practitioners to them.

"While pursuing meditative absorption in such places, it is said to be important to keep the body completely still. Periodically the hermit should arrange his seat outside, covering the ground with piles of fresh and old tree leaves, in an environment filled with scented wildflowers. These youthful blooms of such extreme beauty cannot help but bring a smile; they are the cloud banks of offerings that delight meditators.

"Bees intoxicated on pollen nectar bumble around in these flowers. Happily buzzing about, they provide a pleasant melody.

"The sun naturally illuminates the forest ground where beautiful green shoots and grasses can clearly be seen gleaming like lapis and turquoise. Many herbivorous animals can also be seen, eating shoots and playing in joyful abandon, while overhead, birds of varying sizes fly about and sing their pleasant songs. Such a place is divine indeed, as if a pleasure grove of the heavens had been transported here to earth.

"To take as few as seven steps toward such a pleasant, isolated retreat, one is said to amass great merit. *The Sutra of Dawa Dronme* states:

> Having gone forth from the householder's life, what conduct should be adopted? Give up your obsession with food, drinks, perfumes, clothes, scented flowers and their garlands, and trying to please those in powerful positions. Bring the decaying nature of everything composite to mind and set your sights on buddhahood. Motivated thus, to take just seven steps toward a hermitage will being about extraordinary merit.

Likewise, another sutra states:

> Thinking of retreat and taking seven steps in the direction of a hermitage will cause great merit and propel you to the level of a seventh-ground bodhisattva.

"When young, we spent time listening to and pondering the sublime Dharma. Now that we are a little older, it's time to consider retreats in rocky meadows, in dense groves surrounded by thorny bushes, where the branches of flowery trees such as the tamarisk make an interwoven lattice within which birds make their nests. At the feet of such trees, shy animals such as rabbits and deer can rest and sleep without any cause for concern.

"In winter, face south, as the sun's rays are stronger there, and in summer try to stay cool; awareness is vivid at these times.

"Make sure that you have an easy supply of firewood, water, and other necessities. In these lonely and delightful places, it can be very comfortable to live in a little wooden hut. Reflect how the sages of the past had the fortune to dwell alone and you'll be very happy. *The Sutra of Individual Liberation* says:

> After having received much instruction, to then spend your years living purely in forest retreats is comfort indeed.

Another sutra reads:

> Whosoever dwells in forest retreats will know true joy, as a virtuous life such as this is extremely pleasant.

"Taking care of family and friends, subduing enemies, commerce, farming, and so on, is all very distracting. As is a position in the local town or monastic administration, despite the merit you may make.

"Such distraction isn't a problem if you dwell in a place such as this— the navel of the world, the self-arisen crystal stupa of the great and snowy Mount Kailash, a great mountain whose peak is hidden in white clouds that gently scatter flower-shaped snowflakes. It has the appearance of an open, white parasol. Its sides and slopes are filled with potent medicinal herbs, sweet-smelling incenses, myriad flowers, antelopes, and various kinds of birds such as the divine mountain birds, white grouse, and so on, which continually fly about. Devout pilgrims make their devotions, circumambulations, offerings, prostrations, and so forth, at the foot of the mountain, where you find all the necessities for a successful pilgrimage. It is an extraordinary place of solitude. In places such as these even sleep is very meaningful! Chengawa Lodro Gyaltsen[2] once said:

> With extensive merit gathered from distracting circumstance, to so much as even sleep in such isolation will bring great joy! The ocean of suffering and the ocean of bliss—don't get carried away by the wrong one, O child of the Sakyas.

Je Kalden Gyatso said:

A single act of virtue accomplished in isolated retreat is worth a hundred done with distraction. Having gone into retreat, exert yourself in virtue!

"Should an ordinary person retire to such a place of isolation—where trees are in bloom and laden with fruit, with falls, streams, and grassy meadows with sweet-smelling flowers, where the environment provides sweet foods and potent herbs, where wild animals and birds frolic and play together and sing sweetly to one another without the slightest fear, where there are mountains and valleys blessed by the sublime masters of the past, where awareness is naturally clear—and, inspired by the biographies of the masters of the past, sacrifice having good food, clothing, and pleasant conversation, and have the fortune to sit in a little meditation cabin and earnestly apply himself to practice the instructions received from his master, he will awaken in this very life, in this very body. A sutra reads:

> In the past those who would achieve nirvana retreated to isolated hermitages and there found enlightenment.

The omniscient Longchen Rabjam wrote:

> It is said that the qualities of the buddhas and accomplished ones of the past came from their seclusion. Therefore, I seek mountain retreats.

"Sublime ones have ever practiced only in dense forests such as these, very far from the busyness of the city. Animals wander freely in these beautiful and inspiring places, and, after winters thaw, pure water cascades and flows in abundance, flowers bloom, and various types of bird gather to sing their beautiful songs as they bath and drink in clear, cool pools. Medicinal herbs and fruit of all kinds grow in abundance, each with its own color, taste, and smell; grass is very green and soft, and plenty of trees will offer shade. Aspire and make prayers to go forth from the time-consuming affairs of your life and have the fortune to practice alone here. Shantideva said:

> When shall I come to dwell in forests?
> Among the deer, birds, and trees that say nothing unpleasant and are
>     a delight to be with.[3]

*The Thoughts of Seven Girls* reads:

> May I come to experience the joy of spending my days in the cool shade of a tree, sitting on a mat of soft fresh grass.

The victorious Kalsang Gyatso[4] said:

> People like us should make a heartfelt determination, and pray to be free from the fetters of desire, aspiring to the contemplation and meditation of Dharma in pleasant solitary groves.

Panchen Lobsang Chogyi Gyaltsen said:

> Just as wild geese strain their eyes, anticipating finding wish-
> fulfilling pools beautified with garlands of lotuses,
> Similarly, we should long for the pleasures of solitude from the very
> depths of our hearts.

Jetsun Kalden Gyatso said:

> To aspire and pray to adopt the solitary conduct of a rishi is far better than staying with a few good friends in a pleasant, extremely solitary, mountain retreat.

Jetsun Sakya Rinchen said:

> Sit amid the flowers in forested meadows; peace of mind is found in such wooded dwellings. A great and joyful bliss is won through practicing single-pointed meditation here—the likes of which isn't experienced even in the pleasure groves of the heavens. Dwelling in lonely wilds without tiredness or fatigue, give up all thoughts of quarreling, aggression, stupidity, attachments, and any other mistaken ideas that bring you misery. Decide that you'll stay alone.

"As followers of these past masters, we should hurry to these heavenly mountains whose peaks stretch to the heavens. Brilliant white clouds, like parasols and banners, beautify their shoulders, fog and mist of a silver shade fall around and enwrap their bodies like a curtain, and at their feet are divine green meadows, lush, beautiful, and filled with flowers. The grazing animals of nomads wander throughout the surrounding hills, and herds of wild deer, antelope, and other lovely wild animals freely roam. The tops of the leafy trees are filled with cuckoos, nightingales, and other beautiful birds, all chirping away pleasantly to one another. In the springtime, the younger birds will try to attract a mate and draw her out of her hiding in the deep forest dwelling with enchanting love songs, while bees happily intoxicated on flower nectar buzz around as they gather pollen. Cool waters fall, gurgling down the mountainside, sounding like the joy of a celestial maiden. If hot, go to the sides of the mountain and indulge in the pleasantly cooling waves of the divine fan, cool air that rises and brings sensations of great bliss.

"It has been said time and time again: retire to lonely places of abundance such as these and practice the sublime Dharma. *The Moon Lamp Sutra* reads:

> Give up the delights of towns and villages, and always rely upon the solitude of the forest. Remain alone, like a rhinoceros, and before too long you will win the supreme meditation.

Atisha said:

> Stay far away from places that disturb your mind, and remain in places conducive to virtue. Until stability is won, remain alone in the woodlands; places of distraction are harmful to practice.

The Precious Lord[5] wrote:

> Swarms of bees fly about the myriad flowers that carpet the meadows, their pleasant buzzing is heard from afar. Live as a vagabond; rely upon and awaken in sublime retreats such as these.

Longchenpa stated:

> How wonderful! Those with faith who desire buddhahood, having perfectly entered the highest, greatest secret should enter into retreat by themselves and seize the dharmakaya citadel.

Gyalse Togme wrote:

> When unfavorable places are given up, destructive emotions naturally fade. Without distraction, positive action increases and, as awareness becomes clearer, confidence in the Dharma grows. It is a bodhisattva's practice to rely on solitude.[6]

Chekawa[7] said:

> Child, if you are able to endure the hardships of solitary ascetic practice and live like the sages of old, my work will have been worthwhile.

"Looking at the biographies of the masters of the past, we should strive to emulate them, live in accord with their vajra words, and cut the entanglements that completely ensnare us in the worldly affairs of this life. Live in the mountain solitudes that the sublime masters of the past have praised so highly, wear tattered clothes, eat the worst food, and, above all, practice day and night the vast and profound instructions received from your guru.

> Having thought about birth, death, and the sufferings of samsara,
>     seek out a qualified guru.
> Serve at his feet and receive his instruction—both vast and
>     profound.
> Then, motivated by a wish to awaken, to become Buddha for the sake
>     of all beings, seek out mountain solitude.

> Leave for the tall mountains whose peaks are clad in white cloud,
> A place of nature where clean drinking water cascades down rocky
>     falls,
> Becoming gentle streams that seem to chatter as they gurgle freely
>     along,

> And where foliage and trees, beautified with flowers and laden with
>     fruit,
> Move in great swaying motions, when roused by cool, scented
>     breezes.
> Waving their arms, they call, 'Come and practice meditation here!'

It is said that when meditating, should you wish to sit very still, go to a still place.
Here the hermit lays out his cushion, covering the ground with leaves and twigs, and arranges offerings of fresh, scented flowers to fill the environment.

Bees intoxicated with pollen and nectar bob and dive about, buzzing their little tunes,
Beautiful animals frolic and rest upon the soft green grass,
While birds dip and dive among the branches of the trees, singing their pleasant songs.

Such pleasing and isolated groves, rich and abundant, are like heaven on earth.
To take seven steps toward one is to accrue great merit,
To stay in one will bring happiness, well-being, and renown,
And to stay and practice there will bring buddhahood.

Fortunate disciples of my heart, let us live in accordance with the masters of the past,
Disentangle and detach ourselves from worldly concerns,
And retreat to pleasing places where awareness becomes clearer.
Let's take just the bare necessities and leave everything else behind,
And spend our days and nights exerting ourselves in the practice of the vast and profound instructions we have received!"

## 23

# ENCOURAGEMENT TO ADOPT A NONSECTARIAN OUTLOOK AND CONCLUDING ADVICE

About fifty of my disciples gathered. They included the learned, pure, and most noble Tsegye Lama, the hermit of Ponmo Cave, and many others from the different traditions of Tibetan Buddhism—Sakya, Geluk, Nyingma, Drukpa Kagyu, and so on—all of whom had given up the worldly life to dwell and practice in solitude.

I addressed them, "Fortunate ones, generally the stream of teachings from our kind, compassionate, and most precious Buddha are passed as if lighting many candles from a single flame. In the arya land of India, the teaching spread and came to include the eighteen schools of the shravakas,[1] whereas in the snowy land of Tibet, we find the distinctive flavors of Sakya, Geluk, Nyingma, the Kagyu schools of Drukpa, Drikung, and Dakpo, Shije, Chöd, Jonang, Bodongpa, and so on, each with its unique flavor and yet all committed to the fundamental teaching of Buddha. This much is obvious to a learned person, a well-practiced yogin who through learning and reasoning is familiar with the definitive meaning of Dharma. Should he analyze, he will find that all these traditions come down to a single point. As Amitabha Buddha in the guise of a saffron-clad monk, Panchen Lobsang Chogyi Gyaltsen wrote:

> The Connate Union,[2] Amulet Box,[3] Fivefold,[4] Single Taste,[5] the
> Four Syllables,[6] Pacification,[7] Cutting,[8] the Great Perfection, the
> Quintessential Meditation instructions of Madhyamaka,[9] and
> so on, each has their unique name and presentation, yet when a
> yogin skilled in the definitive meaning through reasoning and
> citation, who also has the experience of practice, investigates, he
> sees that they all come to the same intention.[10]

Drukpa Kunleg said:

> When a learned person looks at Dzogchen, Mahamudra, and Madhyamaka, he sees that they come down to the same thing. Those idiots who reject this, favoring one meditation over another, abandon the Dharma.

And Je Kalden Gyatso said:

> Have conviction in all the different Buddhist traditions of Sakya, Gaden, the earlier or later translations, as they each have profound and sublime methods of awakening.
> Don't denigrate any; rather develop respect for them all.

"It is completely unacceptable to harbor a biased attitude toward the various traditions of Buddhism and those who practice them. These prejudices motivated by the destructive emotions of attachment and aversion lead to biased action, both good and bad. They also lead to contempt and a complete lack of respect toward a particular instruction of Buddha, leading you to criticize it and commit the worst karmic action—abandoning the Dharma. As the lordly Yeshe Gyaltsen stated:

> To think my tradition is correct and that every other position and practice is wrong is the mark of a fool.

The sutras teach that acts of disparaging and abandoning the Dharma result in the most excruciating suffering. They advise avoiding such action even at the cost of your life.

"We should follow this advice along with the four greatnesses of the lamrim teaching as found in Tsongkhapa's *The Great Treatise on the Stages of the Path to Enlightenment*,[11] the greatness of showing how all teachings of Buddha are free from contradiction and of showing how they are all instructions for practice. As the Vajradhara Throne Holder of Reting said:

> To recognize everything that arises in your mind is the mark of a good view. To this effect, we Gelukpas who dwell on Gaden Mountain, our elders, the Nyingmapas, those who live in Sakya, and so on, each have a similar outlook.

Buddha spoke of a similarity in outlook and view; through the practice instructions of the lordly Tsongkhapa, his intent becomes very clear.

"All the different tenet systems and lineages throughout Tibet have a similar intent—they are all instructions of Buddha—and we should develop an unbiased, mutual appreciation for them all. This is very important, as Panchen Lobsang Yeshe[12] said:

> There are many tenets throughout Central Tibet, Tsang, and down into Ngari. All of them are Buddhist; as such do not give strength to the evil devil of sectarianism but rather allow the beautiful jewel light of pure vision to encapsulate them all.

The vidyadhara Gangshar Rangdrol[13] wrote:

> These days there are many Buddhist traditions and tenet systems; they are all, however, the teaching of Buddha and comprise a single path to awakening. Don't throw about your needless criticism. Isn't it better to appreciate them all?

Gwalwong Je[14] said:

> One way to subdue your mind is to develop a nonsectarian and pure view. This training will cause your outlook to become completely unbiased and pure.

Yangonpa mentioned:

> Without clairvoyance, it is very difficult to say who is a sublime person and who isn't. It's far better to avoid insulting anyone, to have a positive outlook, and develop a pure view.

The Venerable Yeshe Gyaltsen said:

> The development of pure view toward all, especially those who practice the Dharma, should be a primary concern for us.

The Victorious Gendun Drup[15] wrote:

Generally, reflect on the kindness of all; and in particular, have a pure outlook toward those who practice the Dharma.

Panchen Lobsang Chogyi Gyaltsen wrote:

On occasion the activities and biographies of the sublime lie beyond the comprehension of us ordinary folk. To avoid the extremely negative actions that arise in dependence upon one's own shortsightedness—particularly that of criticizing and abandoning the exalted ones and their teaching—it is my, Chogyi Gyaltsen's wish, that the jewel light of pure view toward all may come to pervade everywhere.

"To summarize: Buddha, the greatest of spiritual friends, gave the most appropriate instructions to each and every being throughout space. His collected discourse is, as you might imagine, as deep as the oceans—very difficult to fathom.

"Within this vast ocean, some become partial toward one specific teaching and, not understanding the bigger picture, become biased—who would call such a person learned?

"Persons are of varying capacities, some great and others not; based upon these differences, we find a variety of spiritual ways that may seem contradictory at times. Essentially, they are classified into sutra and tantra—a classification within which certain instructions may appear to be in opposition to others. To resolve these issues and see the enlightened intent behind them, it is vital to rely upon the complete word of Buddha, the enlightened commentaries of past masters, and the instructions of your gurus.

"In Tibet, we find much acceptance and rejection of the Buddha's teaching, some good and some bad. We should, however, remember the big picture—the eighty-four thousand instructions—and give up ideas of rejecting the Dharma!

"Some of little aptitude may examine the teachings of Buddha and wonder when will I complete this and realize them all? Such an idea is comparable to an attempt to measure the sky or a thought to pile up stones and reach the sun.

"A doctor doesn't use all his medical knowledge and medicine to cure just one person; he heals them all. Similarly, the discourse of Buddha isn't just for one being; it is for all.

"Just because one teaching doesn't suit a particular individual, it doesn't mean it won't help anyone. There isn't a single teaching of Buddha that's harmful; as such there isn't a single instruction to abandon.

"An instruction that is beneficial for one individual doesn't mean it is helpful for all. Such thought would ruin the application of the Buddha's teaching and would prove harmful for all.

"To quench your thirst, there is no need to drink the entire stream; a few mouthfuls will suffice. Similarly, liberation can be achieved by practicing a few Dharma instructions; there is no need to practice them all.

"'Unless all dharmas are practiced, liberation can't possibly be won!' You may feel this, but you should know that not all of the eighty-four thousand teachings of Buddha were translated into Tibetan. As they'll need to be translated, you'd best set off for India right away!

"For the most part, the learned and realized masters of India and Tibet achieved liberation through the practice of a single instruction. I implore those who cry that they need a hundred such instructions to read the thousands of biographies of the masters of old. Does a single one mention their not achieving liberation?

"Realize that all teachings of Buddha are free from contradiction; allow them all to arise as practical instructions. This way you'll easily find the intent of the Buddha and avoid the greatest of negative actions, the abandonment of the Dharma.

"How wondrous it is, children of my heart, to be harmonious and have an impartial and pure appreciation for all teachings of Buddha; it is like being at a joyous gathering. Having entered the path of the sutras, tantras, and pith instructions, rest assured that your destination, the pleasing city of liberation, is close at hand.

"Having entered the great path of the sutras, tantras, and pith instructions, the pleasant journey to the city of liberation will soon be over.

"At this most sacred of mountains,[16] a place blessed by many accomplished ones, I, the Buddhist practitioner Tsogdruk Rangdrol, have given you, my pure and most fortunate disciples, these sublime teachings."

# 24

## CONCLUSION OF THE TEACHINGS AT KAILASH

I gave these instructions to benefit my disciples at various times during my stay at Kailash, and whatever of the profound and vast Dharma teachings were found useful were written down. These notes were subsequently gathered and laid out in this book—a veritable banquet of instruction. I gave everyone the reading transmission along with an explanation of the entire volume.

At the conclusion, my disciples presented me with many gifts and arranged a ganachakra feast. They said many kind words of praise, combining these with the seven-branch offering prayer of the great elder Atisha:

> Yogin, like a victory banner, you beautify the rooftop of your temple-
>     like disciples,
> With your practice of the three higher trainings as the jewel-tip and
>     your understanding of the three baskets,[1] the eloquent ridge.
>
> Yogin, like a mighty elephant, with the great strength of your altruism
>     and bodhichitta,
> And through the power of your familiarity with the four means of
>     gathering disciples,
> You are exceedingly adept at carrying the responsibility of benefiting
>     the teachings and beings.
>
> Yogin, like the sun, you illuminate the darkness of confusion with the
>     boundless light of vast and profound Dharma radiating from your
>     fiery face.
>
> Yogin, like a sandalwood tree, when the cool breeze of our questions
>     blow,
> The branches and leaves of your fine discrimination wave, bloom, and
>     release the fine, all-permeating scent of your instructions.

Yogin, like an excellent vase, now matter how much you pour the nectar of Dharma—that which causes liberation through taste—from your mouth into your beautiful gold and silver vase-like disciples, it is never exhausted.

Yogin, like a wish-fulfilling tree, the branches of transmitted Dharma spread, laden with the fruit of realization—fulfilling the wishes of your divine disciples.

Yogin, like a lion, with learning, goodness, and nobility perfected, you ruffle your mane of explanation, debate, and composition, while stretching your claws of the four immeasurable thoughts.

Yogin, like a great garuda, hatching from the shell of the twofold obscuration, with your wings of method and wisdom fully formed, you soar in the sky of omniscience.

Yogin, like a turquoise dragon, having gathered clouds of love and concern, you let the Mahayana Dharma thunder forth, causing a soft rain to fall everywhere.
The key of your fine knowledge opens the precious treasury of the Buddha's word,
And you freely dispense whatever is desired; such delight, as if reaching the first bhumi—Supreme Joy!

Lord of the Dharma, so very kind; we offer the accomplishment of our practice to repay you.
From now, until we achieve enlightenment, may we follow and never be separated from you.

*The following verses are the aforementioned seven-branch offering prayer of the great elder Atisha:*

In all lives to come, my I enjoy leisure and fortune and, with marvels complete,
Venerate the three jewels by making offerings and prostrations physically, verbally, and mentally.

With the four powers complete, I confess all previous wrongdoing
and rejoice in all virtue.

I earnestly request you to turn the dharma wheel and request those
about to demonstrate parinirvana to remain.

With prayers of dedication such as these, may all our wishes be
fulfilled.

They went on to offer many prostrations along with other prayers of
dedication.

SHABKAR TSOGDRUK RANGDROL. PHOTOGRAPH COURTESY OF
VEN. MATTHIEU RICARD/SHECHEN ARCHIVE.

## 25

# AFTERWORD

I have beheld the faces and heard the beautiful speech of more than one hundred spiritual friends, including the dharma king Ngakyi Wangpo, the unrivaled holder and disseminator of the teaching of Buddha, Jampel Dorje, he who rendered evident things as they are and thereby knows all, and Jamyang Gyatso, one who has studied so widely that all the teachings of Buddha appear to him as instructions for practice.

All of these gurus poured their nectar-like instructions into this golden receptacle of faith and respect, where the insatiable tongue of discernment savored them.

Having opened manifold treasuries of sutra, tantra, and pith instruction, many important points found their way into the left chuba fold of my mind.

Finding myself rich with these wondrous instructions, both profound and vast, I set off for the delights of lonely, isolated places. Through single-pointed meditation and the blessings of my gurus, experiences and realizations of bodhichitta and more arose in ways I had never experienced before.

The wood and skin of the two collections combined with my pure aspirations gave rise to the illusory form of a great drum—outwardly, just mind, while inwardly, self-liberation of the six-senses.[1] The polite requests of my disciples made up the smooth drumstick, and the drum was gently beaten with respect and gave rise to a pleasant, clear, and uninterrupted melody of the vast and profound Dharma. Wonderful!

This book, *The Emanated Scripture of Manjushri*, appeared within emptiness and luminosity conjoined—the sacred enclosure of my mind. I hereby offer it as a veritable banquet to those of fortune.

The youthful, desirous of happiness, higher states of rebirth, and liberation are easily seduced by the sidelong glances of the attractive instructions of hearing, thinking, and meditation; those who practice the Dharma are right to rely on them.

These fruits of a wish-fulfilling tree, profound and vast instructions, have fallen upon the fertile soil of your minds, my disciples. May they quickly germinate and grow into new wish-fulfilling trees of omniscience, such that all may simultaneously enjoy their fruits.

This book, *The Emanated Scripture of Manjushri*, is based primarily on the peerless writings of Tsongkhapa, the dharma lord of the three realms, and he who is the dance of wisdom personified, Manjushri, appearing in a human guise. He graciously invited the volume that sits upon the lotus that blooms beside Manjushri's left ear into the human realms, of course, the most amazing and wondrous *The Great Treatise on the Stages of the Path to Enlightenment*. I, the hermit Tsogdruk Rangdrol, taught it to many of my fortunate disciples while residing in the Cave of Miracles, on the eastern side of the most majestic of mountains, Mount Kailash—the palace of Chakrasamvara, the dwelling place of 1,500 arhats, and the great gathering place of the dakas and dakinis of the three realms.

To close with a prayer: may the publishers and patrons of this edition of *The Emanated Scripture of Manjushri*—the guru's [Shabkar Tsogdruk Rangdrol's] essential instructions of sutra, tantra, and shastra—have temporal happiness and ultimately awaken to buddhahood.

May anything that is inauspicious such as epidemics, disturbances, and so on, no longer exist, not even in name. And may there be an abundance of food, wealth, prosperity, good harvests, and grain; may auspiciousness and well-being come to pervade all.

# NOTES

## INTRODUCTION BY MATTHIEU RICARD

1. Shabkar Tsogdruk Rangdrol, *The Life of Shabkar: The Autobiography of a Tibetan Yogin*, trans. Matthieu Ricard (Ithaca, NY: Snow Lion Publications, 2001), 307.
2. Ibid., 20.
3. Matthieu Ricard, *The Writings of Shabkar: A Descriptive Catalogue* (New Delhi: Shechen Publications, 2003).
4. Except for two, *The Self-Arising Sun* (*Legs bshad nyi ma rang shar*) and *The Mountain of Gold* (*Gdams ngag gser gyi ri bo*), all of these were composed before the Emanated Scriptures.

## TRANSLATOR'S INTRODUCTION

1. Zhabs dkar tshogs drug rang grol.
2. His teachers were primarily Orgyen Trinley Namgyal (O rgyan 'phrin las rnam rgyal), Jampel Dorje ('Jam dpal rdo rje, d. 1817), and Jamyang Gyatso ('Jam dbyangs rgya mtsho, d. 1800).
3. A rig dge bshes 'jam dpal dge legs rgyal mtsham, 1726–1803. See Shabkar Tsogdruk Rangdrol, *The Life of Shabkar: The Autobiography of a Tibetan Yogin*, trans. Matthieu Ricard (Ithaca, NY: Snow Lion Publications, 2001), xxixn46.
4. Ibid., 43.
5. Ibid., 49n1.
6. The preliminary practices or *ngondro* (*sNgon 'gro*) are the foundational practices of Vajrayana Buddhism. They comprise two parts. The common preliminaries consist of reflection on the preciousness of human life, impermanence, the suffering of the three lower realms of existence, and karma (action, cause-and-effect). The uncommon preliminaries are refuge in the Three Jewels of Buddha, Dharma, and Sangha; taking the pledge of bodhichitta; Vajrasattva meditation; mandala offering; and guru yoga. Each of these preliminaries is carried out a minimum of one hundred thousand times. As such, they are often referred to as the "preliminary practice accumulations." Not only are they accumulated in that they are counted but, more to the point, they add to the accumulation of merit, wisdom, and purification that the average person needs in order to begin Vajrayana practice.
7. Shabkar Tsogdruk Rangdrol, *The Life of Shabkar*, 50.
8. *gSang sngags lam gyi rim pa rin po che gsal ba'i sgron me.*
9. Nyang ral nyi ma 'od zer.
10. *Zhal gdams lam rim ye shes snying po.* A full translation of the poem, titled *Lamrim*

*Yeshe Nyingpo*, can be found along with Jamgon Kongtrul's majestic commentary in Padmasambhava, *The Light of Wisdom*, trans. Erik Pema Kunsang, 4 vols. (Hong Kong: Rangjung Yeshe Publications, 1999).

11. mChog gyur gling pa and 'Jam dbyangs mkhyen brtse'i dbang po.

12. *bDe bar gshegs pa'i bstan pa rin po che la 'jug pa'i lam gyi rim pa* or, as it is commonly referred to, the *bsTan rim chen po* by Gro lung pa, Blo gros 'byung gnas.

13. *Dam chos yid bzhin nor bu thar pa rin po che'i rgyan* by sGam po pa, bSod nams rin chen.

14. *sKal bzang thar ba'i them skas* by 'Khrul zhig o rgyan rnam rgyal (New Delhi: Shechen/Tsadra Publications, 2018).

15. *The Collected Writings of Shabkar* (New Delhi: Shechen Publications, 2003).

## Opening Homage and Prologue

1. The five kinds of degeneration (Tib. *nyigs ma lnga*) are as follows: (1) a degeneration of views due to the decline in the virtue of monastics, (2) degeneration of disturbing emotions due to a decline in the virtue of householders, (3) the degeneration of times due to the decline in enjoyments and an increase in strife, (4) the degeneration of life span due to the decline of the sustaining life force, and (5) the degeneration of sentient beings: a decline of body due to inferior shape and lesser size, a decline of merit due to lesser power and splendor, and a decline of mind due to lesser sharpness of intellect, power of recollection, and diligence.

## Chapter 1: The Necessity of Giving Up the World

1. For a full translation of Shawopa's instruction, see Thupten Jinpa, trans., *The Book of Kadam: The Core Texts* (Somerville, MA: Wisdom Publications, 2008).

## Chapter 3: Identifying a Precious Human Birth

1. That is, to be born in a place which has the fourfold assembly of monks, nuns, and male and female householders.

2. The five heinous actions that result in the immediate transmigration to hell are killing your mother, father, or an arhat, deliberately drawing the blood of the Buddha, and creating a schism in the sangha.

3. The three collections, or baskets, into which the teachings of the Buddha (that is, the Dharma) are divided are ethics, metaphysics, and the discourses or sutras.

## Chapter 4: Death and Impermanence

1. Lit., business, agriculture, and loans.

2. See Jamgön Kongtrul Lodrö Tayé, *The Treasury of Knowledge: Book One: Myriad Worlds* (Ithaca, NY: Snow Lion Publications, 1995) for a description of traditional Buddhist cosmology.

3. Lit., eating, drinking, and chatting with friends.

## CHAPTER 5: BASIC ETHICS

1. *Bodhisattvacaryāvatāra* [The way of the bodhisattva]. Translated into Tibetan as *Byang chub sems dpa'i spyod pa la 'jug pa.*
2. The direct translation of this phrase is for "a male birth."

## CHAPTER 7: THE IMPORTANCE OF ETHICS

1. Nagarjuna, *Suhṛllekha* [Letter to a friend], stanza 7, lines 3 and 4.

## CHAPTER 8: HOW TO ESTABLISH GENUINE COMPASSION

1. Read *dkar* instead of *dkor* as found in both editions. This is a reference to the eight worldly dharmas as black, white, and mixed as found in Shabkar's description. See Shabkar, *Zhab dkar pa'i gur 'bum* [The collected songs of Shabkar].
2. See Jamgön Kongtrul Lodrö Tayé, *The Treasury of Knowledge: Book Eight, Part Four: Esoteric Instructions* (Ithaca, NY: Snow Lion Publications, 2007), 388n38.
3. A *mamo* is a female spirit associated with the natural world. It is easy to upset them through destructive conduct, especially when this involves the disturbance of the environment.
4. *Byang chub lam rim chen mo* [The great treatise on the stages of the path to enlightenment].

## CHAPTER 10: THE CULTIVATION OF BODHICHITTA

1. The above six stanzas are taken from Dharmarakshita, *Mind Training: The Peacock That Destroyed Poison.* For a full translation, see Jinpa, Thupten, trans., *Mind Training: The Great Collection* (Somerville, MA: Wisdom Publications, 2006). For a translation along with a brilliant commentary, see Geshe Lhundup Sopa, with M. J. Sweet and L. Zwilling, *Peacock in the Poison Grove* (Somerville, MA: Wisdom Publications, 2001).

## CHAPTER 11: ON TAKING THE BODHISATTVA'S VOW

1. Here there is a slight difference in wording from the commitment to the awakened mind (bodhichitta) as found in the Shantideva, *Bodhisattvacaryāvatāra* [The way of the bodhisattva], chap. 2, vv. 23–24. Both the mTsho sngo mi rigs dpe skunk khang and Zhe chen editions have the same wording thereby negating the notion of a simple miscopy. The meaning remains identical. See Shantideva, *The Way of the Bodhisattva*, trans. Padmakara Translation Group (Boulder, CO: Shambhala Publications, 2006). The following two verses of dedication are identical to those found in *The Way of the Bodhisattva.*

## CHAPTER 12: THE BODHISATTVA'S VOW

1. The twelve scriptural references are general teachings, hymns and praises, prophecies, teachings in verse, aphorisms, pragmatic narratives, biographical narrative, narratives with former events serving as examples, narratives of former lives, extensive teachings, narratives through miracles, and the teaching of profound doctrines.

2. The five sciences are spiritual philosophy, logic and dialectics, grammar, medicine, and mechanical arts and crafts.

## Chapter 15: Methods for Achieving Special Insight

1. Tsegya Monastery is the only monastery on the banks of Lake Rakkas Tsa, near Mount Kailash.
2. The four ways, or means, of attracting and gathering disciples are to be generous, to speak pleasingly, to teach what is needed, and to act in accordance with the teachings given. See chapter 12.
3. The three powers or qualities of a mature lion are the power to make a small jump with precision, to make a long jump, and to leap through space.
4. These verses are taken from the Ngawang Lobsang Gyatso, the Fifth Dalai Lama, *Byang chub lam gyi rim pa'i khrid yig 'jam pa'i dbyangs kyi zhal lung* [The words of Manjushri], a lam-rim text.

## Chapter 16: The Need for Both Calm Abiding and Special Insight

1. Bon-ri is a mountain sacred to the Bonpos, near Lake Manasarovar in Kong po. On its northeast side, there is a seat of the Gelukpa school that was founded by the great meditator Khedrub Lobsang Norbu (mKhas grub blo bzang nor bu). The tulku referred to here may be his reincarnation.
2. The actual word used is "Sahor" (Za hor), which is a degenerate form of a word in an Indian dialect referring to Bengal. See Jinpa, *Mind Training*, 581n42, for a very useful etymological look at the word.
3. The five sciences are language, logic and reasoning, medicine, arts and craft, and religious philosophy.
4. The three baskets (*tripitaka*) are ethics (*vinaya*), metaphysics (*abhidharma*), and the discourses (*sutra*).
5. The four classes of tantra are action (*kriya*), performance (*charya*), yoga (*yoga*), and highest yoga (*anuttara yoga*).
6. *Samādhisaṃbhāraparivarta* [The requisites for meditative stabilization chapter], translated into Tibetan as *Ting nge 'dzin tshogs kyi le'u*, written by one of Atisha's teachers, Bodhibhadra (Byang chub bzang po). See Geshe Sonam Rinchen and Ruth Sonam, *Atisha's Lamp for the Path to Enlightenment* (Ithaca, NY: Snow Lion Publications, 1997), 205n4.
7. For the complete list, along with an explanation, see Geshe Sonam Rinchen and Ruth Sonam, *Atisha's Lamp*, 93–96.
8. The thirteen requisites are (1) the five forms of fulfillment that relate to oneself, (2) the five forms of fulfillment that relate to others, (3) the aspiration to develop virtuous qualities, (4) the restraint gained through morality, (5) the restraint of the senses, (6) regulating the amount of one's food, (7) striving to remain wakeful during the first and last periods of the night, (8) abiding in a state of vigilance, (9) reliance upon a spiritual teacher, (10) listening to and reflecting upon the true Dharma, (11) remaining free of inner and outer obstacles, (12) being generous, and (13) acquiring the ornaments of a spiritual ascetic.

9. The first of four paths that make up the path of preparation. The other three are peak, acceptance, and supreme heat.

10. The first of the ten bodhisattva grounds. The other nine are Stainless, Luminous, Radiant, Difficult to Overcome, Manifest, Gone Afar, Immovable, Fine Intelligence, and the Cloud of Dharma.

11. The first of four paths that comprise the path of preparation.

12. The first of the ten bodhisattva grounds (*bhumis*).

### CHAPTER 18: ULTIMATE BODHICHITTA

1. The three doors to liberation are emptiness, the absence of characteristics, and the absence of aspiration.

2. This and the following quotes of Milarepa are found in his *Mi la ras pa'i mgur 'bum* [The collected songs of Milarepa].

### CHAPTER 19: MAHAMUDRA

1. The first two lines of a four-line praise to the Perfection of Wisdom.

2. These are the first words that the historical Buddha, Shakyamuni, uttered after awakening.

### CHAPTER 20: BUDDHAHOOD WITHOUT MEDITATION

1. From Saraha, *Dohakośa* [Treasury of song], translated into Tibetan as *gLu mdzod*. For an English translation of this poem, see Edward Conze, I. B. Horner, David Snellgrove, and Arthur Waley, trans., *Buddhist Texts through the Ages* (London: One World Publications, 2014). The rest of this chapter is loosely based upon this poem.

2. This is a reference to the ten powers of Buddha: (1) knowing what is possible and what is not possible, (2) knowing the results of actions, (3) knowing the aspirations of people, (4) knowing the elements, (5) knowing the higher and lower powers of people, (6) knowing the path that leads everywhere, (7) knowing the origin of kleshas, which leads to meditation, liberation, samadhi, and equanimity, (8) knowing previous lives, (9) knowing of transference and death, and (10) knowing that the defilements are exhausted.

3. *bDe mchog mkha' 'gro'i snyan rgyud.* Part of the ear-whispered tradition of Rechungpa.

4. Aryadeva, *Catuḥśataka* [Four hundred stanzas on the middle way], translated into Tibetan as *Byor spyod pa bzhi brgya pa.* For an English translation, see Ruth Sonam and Geshe Sonam Rinchen, trans., *Aryadeva's "Four Hundred Stanzas on the Middle Way"* (Ithaca, NY: Snow Lion Publications, 2008), v. 191.

5. *Phag mo gru pa rdo rje rgyal po.*

6. *Lhan cig skyes sbyor go cha*, in Phagmo Drupa's collected writings, vol. 4 (Kathmandu: Nepal: Sri Gautam Buddha Vihara, 2016).

7. Possibly a reference to Buddha Dipamkara, the third buddha of this fortunate aeon.

8. A reference to the eight "common" accomplishments that arise through this type of meditation: celestial land, sword, pill, swift feet, vase, yaksha, elixir, and eye lotion.

9. These verses are from *Le'u bdun ma* [The prayer to Guru Rinpoche in seven chapters].

10. Found in the *Padma bka' thang*, a terma of Orgyan Lingpa

11. *Bodhisattvacaryāvatāra* [The way of the bodhisattva], translated into Tibetan as *Byang chub sems pa'i spyod pa la 'jug pa*.

## CHAPTER 22: THE BENEFIT OF RETREAT

1. The eight worldly concerns are hope for happiness, fame, praise, and gain, and fear of suffering, insignificance, blame, and loss.
2. An early Gelukpa master, a disciple of Khedrup Gelek Palzang.
3. *Bodhisattvacaryāvatāra* [The way of the bodhisattva], chap. 8, v. 25.
4. The Seventh Dalai Lama.
5. An epithet for Tsongkhapa.
6. *rGyal sras lag len so bdun ma* [The thirty-seven practices of a bodhisattva].
7. Kadampa Geshe Chekawa Yeshe Drove (Chad kha pa ye shes rdo rje).

## CHAPTER 23: ENCOURAGEMENT TO ADOPT A NONSECTARIAN OUTLOOK AND CONCLUDING ADVICE

1. A division into eighteen schools based on different interpretations of the vinaya. It is generally accepted that the differences of interpretation became apparent during the third Buddhist council in the third century BCE.
2. The Mahamudra instructions of Gampopa.
3. The Mahamudra instructions of Khyungpo Naljor that are handed down through the Shangpa Kagyu.
4. The fivefold Mahamudra, primarily practiced in the Drikung Kagyu, which is based on the teachings of Phagmo Drupa and Jigten Sumgön.
5. A set of six meditations hidden by Rechungpa and later discovered by Tsangpa Gyare. They are found within the five unique teachings of the Drukpa Kagyu, and make up "conduct."
6. The Four Syllables Mahamudra, a style of presenting Mahamudra received by Marpa in a dream about Saraha.
7. From the meditation instructions of Padampa Sangye.
8. The instructions of Machig Labdron.
9. Pith instructions for meditating on emptiness found primarily within the Kadam and Gelukpa traditions.
10. *dGe ldan bka' brgyud rin po che'i bka' srol phyag rgya chen po'i rtsa ba rgyas par bshad pa yang gsal sgrom me* [The brilliant lamp: Commentary to the Gaden Kagyu Mahamudra]. For an English translation, see H. H. the Dalai Lama and Alexander Berzin, *The Gelug/Kagyü Tradition of Mahamudra* (Ithaca, NY: Snow Lion Publications, 1997).
11. These are four reasons that show the greatness of the stages of the path to enlightenment: the greatness of showing how all teachings of Buddha are free from contradiction, of showing how they are all instructions for practice, of enabling one to easily find the intent of Buddha, and the greatness in holding one from great wrongdoing.
12. The Second Panchen Rinpoche.
13. Another name for the Fifth Dalai Lama.

14. *rGyal dbang rje*, a great master of the Drukpa Kagyu.
15. The First Dalai Lama.
16. Mount Kailash, where the teachings were given. See Shabkar Tsogdruk Rangdrol, *The Life of Shabkar*, 275.

## CHAPTER 24: CONCLUSION OF THE TEACHINGS AT KAILASH

1. The three baskets of abhidharma, sutra, and vinaya.

## CHAPTER 25: AFTERWORD

1. A play on Shabkar's name: Tsogdruk Rangdrol, Self-Liberation of the Six Senses.

# Bibliography

## Works in English

Conze, Edward, Horner, I. B., Snellgrove, David, and Waley, Arthur., trans. *Buddhist Texts through the Ages*. London: One World Publications, 2014.

Engle, Artemus B., trans. *The Bodhisattva Path to Unsurpassed Enlightenment*. Boulder, CO: Snow Lion, 2016.

Geshe Lhundup Sopa, with M. J. Sweet and L. Zwilling. *Peacock in the Poison Grove*. Somerville, MA: Wisdom Publications, 2001.

Geshe Sonam Rinchen and Ruth Sonam. *Atisha's Lamp for the Path to Enlightenment*. Ithaca, NY: Snow Lion Publications, 1997.

Gyalwa Kalzang Gyatso, the Seventh Dalai Lama. *Songs of Spiritual Change*. Translated by Glenn Mullin. Ithaca, NY: Gabriel/Snow Lion Publications, 1982.

H. H. the Dalai Lama and Alexander Berzin. *The Gelug/Kagyü Tradition of Mahamudra*. Ithaca, NY: Snow Lion Publications, 1997.

Hopkins, Jeffrey, trans. and ed. *Nāgārjuna's Precious Garland: Buddhist Advice for Living and Liberation*. Ithaca, NY: Snow Lion Publications, 2007.

Jamgön Kongtrul Lodrö Tayé. *The Treasury of Knowledge: Book One: Myriad Worlds*. Ithaca, NY: Snow Lion Publications, 1995.

———. *The Treasury of Knowledge: Book Eight, Part Four: Esoteric Instructions*. Ithaca, NY: Snow Lion Publications, 2007.

Jinpa, Thupten, trans. *Mind Training: The Great Collection*. Somerville, MA: Wisdom Publications 2006.

———, trans. *The Book of Kadam: The Core Texts*. Somerville, MA: Wisdom Publications, 2008.

Padmasambhava. *Lamrim Yeshe Nyingpo*. In *The Light of Wisdom*, translated by Erik Pema Kunsang. 4 vols. Hong Kong: Rangjung Yeshe Publications 1999.

Ricard, Matthieu. *The Writings of Shabkar: A Descriptive Catalogue*. New Delhi: Shechen Publications, 2003.

Shabkar Tsogdruk Rangdrol. *The Life of Shabkar: The Autobiography of a Tibetan Yogin*. Translated by Matthieu Ricard. Ithaca, NY: Snow Lion Publications, 2001.

Shantideva. *The Way of the Bodhisattva*. Translated by the Padmakara Translation Group. Boulder, CO: Shambhala Publications, 2006.

## SUTRAS

*Ārya-akṣayamati-nirdeśa-nāma-mahāyāna-sūtra* [Akṣayamati sutra]. Translated into Tibetan as *bLo gros mi zad pa'i bstan pa theg pa chen po'i mdo.*

*Ārya-bodhisattva-piṭaka* [The bodhisattva basket sutra]. Translated into Tibetan as *Byang chub sems dpa'i sde snod.*

*Ārya-dharma-saṃgīti-nāma-mahāyāna-sūtra* [Compendium of the teachings sutra]. Translated into Tibetan as *Chos yang dag par sdud pa'i mdo.*

*Ārya-gayā-śirṣa-nāma-mahāyāna-sūtra* [Foremost of Gaya sutra]. Translated into Tibetan as *'Phags pa ga ya go ri'i theg pa chen po'i mdo.*

*Ārya-mañjuśrī-vikurvāṇa-parivarta-nāma-mahāyāna-sūtra* [The chapter on the miracles of Manjushri]. Translated into Tibetan as *'Phags pa 'jam dpal rnam par 'phrul pa'i le'u zhe bya theg pa chen po'i mdo.*

*Ārya-prajñāpāramitā-sañcayagāthā* [The condensed perfection of wisdom sutra]. Translated into Tibetan as *'Phags pa shes rab kyi pha rol tu phyin pa sdud pa tshigs su bcad pa.*

*Ārya-śraddhā-balādhānāvatāra-nāma-mahāyāna-sūtra* [Seal of engaging in developing the power of faith sutra]. Translated into Tibetan as *'Phags pa dad pa'i stobs bskyed pa theg pa chen po'i mdo.*

*Avataṃsaka-sūtra* [The flower ornament sutra]. Translated into Tibetan as *mDo sde sdong bo bkod pa.*

*Avikalpapraveśadhāraṇī* [Mnemonic, entering the nonconceptual]. Translated into Tibetan as *rNam par mi rtog pa la 'jug pa'i gzungs.*

*Candrapradīpa-sūtra* [The sutra of Dawa Dronme]. Translated into Tibetan as *Zla ba sgron me'i mdo.* Also known as *Samādhirāja sūtra.*

*Gaṇḍavyūha-sūtra* [Chapter 8 of the flower ornament sutra]. Translated into Tibetan as *sDong po bkod pa'i mdo.*

*Mahāparinirvāṇa-sūtra* [The nirvana sutra]. Translated into Tibetan as *Mya ngan las 'das pa'i mdo.*

*Prātimokṣa-sūtra* [The sutra of individual liberation]. Translated into Tibetan as *So thar gyi mdo.*

*Sāgaramatiparipṛcchā-sūtra* [The question of Lodro Gyatso sutra]. Translated into Tibetan as *Blo gros rgya mtshos zhu pa'i mdo.*

*Samādhirāja-sūtra* [The king of concentration sutra]. Translated into Tibetan as *Ting nge 'dzin gyi rgyal po'i mdo.*

[The sutra that discriminates between the paths of virtue and sin]. Translated into Tibetan as *dGe sdig rnam par 'byed pa'i mdo.*

[The teaching of the Buddha's sneeze]. Translated into Tibetan as *Sangs rgyas kyi sbrid pa sangs pa'i sgra.*

## TANTRAS

*Prāddhaka-ānīra-a* (in the language of Oddiyana) [The tantra that causes liberation through contact]. Translated into Tibetan as *bTags grol gyi rgyud*.

*Ratna kūṭa mahā guṇoddeśa tantra raja* [The heap of jewels tantra]. Translated into Tibetan as *Rin po che spungs po'i rgyud*.

*Ratnākara śabda mahā prasaṅga tantra* [The reverberation of sound tantra]. Translated into Tibetan as *sGra thal 'gyur rtsa ba'i rgyud*.

*Sekoddeśa* [The abridged empowerment]. Translated into Tibetan as *dBang mdor bstan pa*.

*Subāhu-paripṛcchā-tantrā* [The tantra requested by Subahu]. Translated into Tibetan as *dPung bzang gis zhus pa'i rgyud*.

*Vairocanābhisaṃbodhi-tantra* [Tantra of Vairochana's enlightenment]. Translated into Tibetan as *rNam snang mngon byang rgyud*.

## SANSKRIT AND TIBETAN TREATISES

Arya Dewa Dzepa. *sPyod bsdus sgron me* [The summary of conduct].

Aryadeva. *Catuḥśataka* [Four hundred stanzas on the middle way]. Translated into Tibetan as *Byor spyod pa bzhi brgya pa*.

Asanga. *Bodhisattvabhūmi* [The bodhisattva grounds]. Translated into Tibetan as *Byang sa*. English translation in Artemus B. Engle, trans. *The Bodhisattva Path to Unsurpassed Enlightenment*. Boulder, CO: Snow Lion, 2016.

———. *Śrāvakabhūmi* [Hearer levels]. Translated into Tibetan as *Nyan thos kyi sa*.

Atisha. *Bodhipathapradīpa* [A lamp for the path to enlightenment]. Translated into Tibetan as *Byang chub lam sgron*.

Atisha and Dromtonpa. *bKa' gdams glegs bam* [The book of Kadam].

*bDe mchog mkha' 'gro'i snyan rgyud* [The ear-whispered tradition of the dakini Chakrasambhava].

Bodhibhadra. *Samādhisaṃbhāraparivarta* [The requisites for meditative stabilization chapter]. Translated into Tibetan as *Ting nge 'dzin tshogs kyi le'u*.

Chengawa Lodro Gyaltsen. *Thog ma'i blo sbyong* [Opening the door to the Dharma: The initial greater vehicle mind training instructions].

Dorje Gyalpo. *Lhan cig skyes sbyor go cha*. In Phagmo Drupa's collected writings, vol. 4. Kathmandu, Nepal: Sri Gautam Buddha Vihara, 2016.

———. *Phag mo gru pa rdo rje rgyal po*.

Gyalse Togme Zangpo. *rGyal sras lag len so bdun ma* [The thirty-seven practices of a bodhisattva].

Kalsang Gyatso, the Seventh Dalai Lama. *gDams pa dang snyan mgur phyogs gcig tu bkod pa* [The collected songs of Kalsang Gyatso, the Seventh Dalai Lama].

Kamalashila. *Bhāvanākrama* [The first and larger stages of meditation]. Translated into Tibetan as *sGom rim dang po*.

———. *Bhāvanākrama* [The middle-length stages of meditation]. Translated into Tibetan as *sGom rim bar pa.*

Lobsang Yeshe, the Second Panchen Lama. *Lam gyi rim pa'i dmar khrid thams cad mkhen par bgrod pa'i myur lam* [The swift path].

Milarepa. *Mi la ras pa'i mgur 'bum* [The collected songs of Milarepa].

Nagarjuna. *Mūlamadhyamakakārikā* [The root verses on the middle way]. Translated into Tibetan as *dBu ma rtsa ba shes rab.*

———. *Ratnāvali* [The precious garland]. Translated into Tibetan as *Rin chen phreng ba.*

———. *Suhṛllekha* [Letter to a friend]. Translated into Tibetan as *bShes springs.*

———. *Śūnyatāsaptatikārikā* [Seventy stanzas on emptiness]. Translated into Tibetan as *sTong nyid bdun cu pa.*

Ngawang Lobsang Gyatso, the Fifth Dalai Lama. *bLo sbyong legs bshad kun 'dus* [The mind training compendium of excellent sayings].

———. *Byang chub lam gyi rim pa'i khrid yig 'jam pa'i dbyangs kyi zhal lung* [The words of Manjushri].

*Nges don phyag chen rgya gzhung* [The collected Indian treatises on the Mahamudra of definitive meaning].

Orgyan Lingpa. *Padma bka' thang.* Terma.

Padmasambhava. *Le'u bdun ma* [The prayer to Guru Rinpoche in seven chapters].

———. *mKha' gro snying thig* [The heart essence of the dakini].

Palgon Pema Vajra. *Śrī Guhyasiddhi.* Translated into Tibetan as *dPal gsang ba grub pa.*

Panchen Lobsang Chogyi Gyaltsen. *dGe ldan bka' brgyud rin po che'i bka' srol phyag rgya chen po'i rtsa ba rgyas par bshad pa yang gsal sgrom me* [The brilliant lamp: Commentary to the Gaden Kagyu Mahamudra].

Potawa. *Po to ba'i gsung sgros* [The collected sayings of Potawa].

Shantideva. *Bodhisattvacaryāvatāra* [The way of the bodhisattva]. Translated into Tibetan as *Byang chub sems dpa'i spyod pa la 'jug pa.*

Saraha. *Dohakośa* [Treasury of song]. Translated into Tibetan as *gLu mdzod.*

Shabkar. *Zhab dkar pa'i gur 'bum* [The collected songs of Shabkar].

Tsongkhapa. *Byang chub lam rim chen mo* [The great treatise on the stages of the path to enlightenment].

# INDEX

*Hri* *Great Protector emanated from the heart of Samantabhadra,*
*majestic master of subjugation, and sovereign of all.*
*Praise to you who controls the three realms!*

Gonkar, literally the "White Protector," is the principal protector of
Kunzang Dechen Gyalpo's terma the
*Wish-Fulfilling Gem: The Union of Hayagriva and Varahi*—
Shabkar's main practice. Drawing by Chris Banigan.